BASIC TEXTS IN COUNSELLING AND PSYCHOTHERAPY

Series editor: Stephen Frosh

This series introduces readers to the theory
psychotherapy across a wide range of topic
wishing to use counselling and psychothera
relevant to workers in health, education, so

D1524910

books are unusual in being rooted in psychodynamic and systemic ideas, yet
being written at an accessible, readable and introductory level. Each text offers
theoretical background and guidance for practice, with creative use of clinical
examples.

Published

Jenny Altschuler
COUNSELLING AND PSYCHOTHERAPY FOR FAMILIES IN TIMES OF ILLNESS AND
DEATH 2nd Edition

Bill Barnes, Sheila Ernst and Keith Hyde
AN INTRODUCTION TO GROUPWORK

Stephen Briggs
WORKING WITH ADOLESCENTS AND YOUNG ADULTS 2nd Edition

Alex Coren
SHORT-TERM PSYCHOTHERAPY 2nd Edition

Jim Crawley and Jan Grant
COUPLE THERAPY

Emilia Dowling and Gill Gorell Barnes
WORKING WITH CHILDREN AND PARENTS THROUGH SEPARATION AND
DIVORCE

Loretta Franklin
AN INTRODUCTION TO WORKPLACE COUNSELLING

Gill Gorell Barnes
FAMILY THERAPY IN CHANGING TIMES 2nd Edition

Fran Hedges
AN INTRODUCTION TO SYSTEMATIC THERAPY WITH INDIVIDUALS

Fran Hedges
REFLEXIVITY IN THERAPEUTIC PRACTICE

John Hills
INTRODUCTION TO SYSTEMIC AND FAMILY THERAPY

Sally Hodges
COUNSELLING ADULTS WITH LEARNING DISABILITIES

Linda Hopper
COUNSELLING AND PSYCHOTHERAPY WITH CHILDREN AND ADOLESCENTS

Sue Kegerreis
PSYCHODYNAMIC COUNSELLING WITH CHILDREN AND YOUNG PEOPLE

Ravi Rana
COUNSELLING STUDENTS

Tricia Scott
INTEGRATIVE PSYCHOTHERAPY IN HEALTHCARE

Geraldine Shipton
WORKING WITH EATING DISORDERS

Laurence Spurling
AN INTRODUCTION TO PSYCHODYNAMIC COUNSELLING 2nd Edition

Paul Terry
COUNSELLING AND PSYCHOTHERAPY WITH OLDER PEOPLE 2nd Edition

Jan Wiener and Mannie Sher
COUNSELLING AND PSYCHOTHERAPY IN PRIMARY HEALTH CARE

Shula Wilson
DISABILITY, COUNSELLING AND PSYCHOTHERAPY

Steven Walker
CULTURALLY COMPETENT THERAPY

Jenny Walters
WORKING WITH FATHERS

Jessica Yakeley
WORKING WITH VIOLENCE

Invitation to authors

The Series Editor welcomes proposals for new books within the Basic Texts in Counselling and Psychotherapy series. These should be sent to Stephen Frosh at the School of Psychology, Birkbeck College, Malet Street, London, WC1E 7HX (e-mail s.frosh@bbk.ac.uk)

Basic Texts in Counselling and Psychotherapy
Series Standing Order ISBN 0–333–69330–2
(outside North America only)

You can receive future titles in this series as they are published by placing a standing order. Please contact your bookseller or, in the case of difficulty, write to us at the address below with your name and address, the title of the series and the ISBN quoted above.

Customer Services Department, Macmillan Distribution Ltd
Houndmills, Basingstoke, Hampshire RG21 6XS, England

Working with Trauma

Systemic Approaches

GERRILYN SMITH

Senior Consultant,
Clinical Psychologist and Systemic Psychotherapist

palgrave
macmillan

First published 2013 by
PALGRAVE MACMILLAN

Palgrave Macmillan in the UK is an imprint of Macmillan Publishers
Limited, registered in England, company number 785998, of Houndmills,
Basingstoke, Hampshire RG21 6XS.

Palgrave Macmillan in the US is a division of St Martin's Press LLC,
175 Fifth Avenue, New York, NY 10010.

Palgrave Macmillan is the global academic imprint of the above companies
and has companies and representatives throughout the world.

Palgrave® and Macmillan® are registered trademarks in the United States,
the United Kingdom, Europe and other countries

ISBN 978–0–230–23649–3

This book is printed on paper suitable for recycling and made from fully
managed and sustained forest sources. Logging, pulping and manufacturing
processes are expected to conform to the environmental regulations of the
country of origin.

A catalogue record for this book is available from the British Library.

A catalog record for this book is available from the Library of Congress.

10   9   8   7   6   5   4   3   2   1
22 21 20 19 18 17 16 15 14 13

Printed and bound in Great Britain by
CPI Antony Rowe, Chippenham and Eastbourne

To My Father
Captain Reginald Smith
16 September 1934 – 5 March 2012
Sans Amertume

Contents

CONTENTS

PREFACE

This book has taken a long time to manifest. It has been overtaken by life events that interrupted the attention and focus needed to complete such a project. In part this underlines the intention of the book to focus on the interaction between the passage of time and lived experience, including traumatic events.

Although my voice is predominant, there are many other voices woven into the text. I have tried to be respectful of the personal experience shared and mindful that the purpose of the book is not to overwhelm or traumatise the reader. The cases supporting the theoretical material are taken from clinical practice. Aspects and details have been changed to protect client confidentiality, as the material touches on private painful experiences. This has been done in discussion with many of the clients who have shared their stories and through therapeutic work for this publication.

This book is intended to be a reader in trauma; to move between theory and practice. As Paolo Bertrando (2007, p. 4) states 'theory is useless if not embedded in practice; and practice is superficial if not grounded in theory'. It spans three decades of clinical work. Writing this book has provided an opportunity to reflect on my practice – it represents my inner voices (Rober, 2005) now made public in the hope that this sharing acts as an inspiration or catalyst to new ways of thinking and working with trauma.

It is the 'algorithm of my heart' (Bateson, 1973, p. 112) and as such has been difficult to translate. I subscribe to the view that 'knowledge does not represent an "objective" ontological reality, but exclusively an ordering and organisation of a world constructed by our experience' (Glasersfeld in Flemons, 1991, p. 55).

I have selected references that resonate with my practice and practice that resonates with current theories. What is presented is the lived experience and evolution of my professional practice interwoven around the theme of trauma and resilience.

In discussion with Stephen Frosh, I wanted to write a book that looked at these concepts from a systemic perspective, reflecting life-cycle issues. It is my perception that trauma is very much a focus of clinical interventions but that the discourse has currently been hijacked by the brain, at the expense of the body and soul and the collective communal spaces they inhabit. Clinical discussions can be focused on problems or symptoms and frequently ignore the acts of resilience and resistance that coexist with a traumatic experience.

My own professional journey covers many life-cycle issues. There are times when I have been seduced by rational, logical, scientific explanations of trauma at the expense of my body and soul. Writing this book has focused my attention on the thinking and feeling that goes on in therapy. I am reminded that intellectual 'rigour alone is paralytic death, but imagination alone is insanity' (Flemons, 1991, p. 41). I hope I have walked the line between paralysis and insanity with delicacy, grace and good humour.

In describing my own journey as a systemic psychotherapist, I was influenced strongly by my teachers at the Tavistock Clinic who encouraged me in my irreverence and slightly anarchic approach – most notably David Campbell and Gill Gorell Barnes. At the time I was studying with them I was actively involved in the women's movement, feminist politics and the London Rape Crisis Centre. This was my trauma front line.

In some strange symmetry Gregory Bateson's *Steps to an Ecology of Mind* (1973) sits beside Mary Daly's *Gyn/Ecology: The Metaethics of Radical Feminism* (1978); Shulamith Firestone's *The Dialectic of Sex: The Case for Feminist Revolution* (1979) beside Paolo Bertrando's *The Dialogical Therapist* (2007), on my bookshelf. This reflects my stochastic learning process.

I am sharing both 'writings from inside the event' and 'those skewed by the distorting lens of retrospective recollection and selective memory' (Kassow, 2007, p. 13).

In considering life-cycle issues in trauma work, I am indirectly looking at my own life-cycle issues as a systemic psychotherapist. I can remember a time when I would not have called myself a 'therapist' at all – as 'those seven letters mean both one who heals and one who rapes' (Smith, 1987). I have chosen to use clinician throughout the text in preference.

I continue to work with an 'awareness and sensitivity to levels of context and meaning – how they interconnect in intricate and often paradoxical ways' (Flemons, 1991, p. 3).This book attempts to combine thinking, feelings and reflections from a wide range of sources; schools of thought and practice.

It examines 'layered networks of premises and patterns of circular interactions within and between ideas and people' (Flemons, 1991, p. 16). Trauma stories are monologic – frozen narratives (Blow and Daniel, 2002). Trauma time is flat time – recursive without reflexivity. Resilience, in contrast, is like water, it flows around and seeps into every nook and cranny seeking the source – expansive yet penetrating. How can we remember to forget? (Flemons, 1991, p. 137).

All words in **bold** appear in the glossary to help orient the reader to unfamiliar terms or concepts.

INTRODUCTION

The book is divided into three parts. Part 1 is 'The Gateway to Practice'. Two theoretical issues, diagnostics and resiliencies, have been selected as broad themes for discussion.

Chapter 1 focuses on the issue of diagnostic labels, specifically psychiatric labels, for emotional states that often follow from traumatic events. The chapter discusses the *Diagnostic and Statistical Manual of Mental Disorders* (DSM) (American Psychiatric Association, 2000), the *International Statistical Classification of Diseases and Related Health Problems* (ICD) (2007) and the concept of post traumatic stress disorder (PTSD). The role and function of a diagnosis is examined as part of identity formation. In some cases it becomes both a colonisation of lived experience and a 'totalising identity', leaving no room for other healthy aspects of self to be visible and/or viable. The chapter examines how diagnostic labels can be used within systemic work as a vehicle to explore aspects of identity rather than as an end in themselves.

In Chapter 2 resiliencies, in the plural, are discussed, encouraging clinicians to consider the multiple contexts in which clients live that contribute to (or inhibit) their ability to enjoy a good quality of life despite adversity. The move towards emotional wellbeing as the focus of clinical intervention is a reflection of the rising importance of the discourses of health and illness.

Part 2, 'The Field of Practice', focuses on clinical work. Three clinical themes have been selected: engagement and creating a safe context, stories we tell ourselves, and working systemically with PTSD symptoms.

The case examples come from my clinical practice. Overwhelmingly this involves relational trauma. My professional experience of trauma work began in the late 1970s with sexual violence, specifically rape. This led to work in child sexual abuse and came to include other safeguarding issues like domestic violence, neglect and physical abuse.

I have worked throughout my career with children, young people and adults who spent time in the 'care system'. This led me to a number of specific client groups. As part of a large scale investigation I interviewed men abused in the 'Approved Schools' and residential units in north-west England and Wales. More recently I have been involved with Irish Care survivors from the orphanages abused by religious people entrusted with their upbringing.

I have worked in child and adolescent mental health services (CAMH) for most of my career. These client groups span the life cycle from babies to grandparents; males and females; mostly but not exclusively white; and predominantly but not exclusively heterosexual. Common themes and patterns emerged in hearing these stories which I have synthesised into this book in the hope of informing theory and practice within relational trauma specifically, but also perhaps trauma generally.

I have used the techniques described in this book with other types of traumatic experience including war and medical interventions; however, I wanted to remain within my primary area of expertise and depth of experience. I have not drawn attention to race or class specifically. Ethnicity or cultural identity can be assumed by names; however, these have been randomly selected and allocated to the material which has been modified to protect client confidentiality. The intention of sharing clinical material is to support theoretical ideas and enhance clinical practice. Cross-cultural competence is essential when working outside of your own cultural identity. However, not belonging to a community can be helpful when dealing with a traumatic experience that is closely connected to that community. For example, in working with Asian women who have experienced domestic violence my not belonging to the community has provided additional protection for them. I received cultural consultation from Asian women's groups and on occasions jointly worked cases with refuge workers. Similarly, working with interpreters adds subtlety, depth and nuance to clinical work.

The clinical material is presented in a variety of forms – some retrospectively as clinical vignettes; extracts from letters and diaries; transcripts of sessions. They run across the life cycle, from the unborn child and newborn considered too young to remember, to grandparents considered too old to forget.

Part 3, 'The Practice Neighbourhood', focuses on wider systems including family, friends and community; and the importance of supervision. These topics are presented through the lens of my own professional journey. This includes important life-cycle issues – the transitions we make in our life journey from child to adult; childless to parent to grandparent; single, married, divorced; through illness and health.

These are all passages which provide us with a different vantage point to view lived experiences – our own and others.

Our professional identities locate us within our communities and families – sometimes uncomfortably. Continuing professional development needs to consider how our work influences both our personal and professional identities. Specialising in trauma will increase your exposure to disturbing material but it may also encourage you to find better ways of managing the personal and professional boundary. It can provoke profound lifestyle changes, as you share with your clients the journey to find meaning and recover hope. It may encourage you to develop a spiritual practice.

Our remembered experiences play across our lives; different aspects shaping what is recalled as and when necessary. We remember for a reason. Remembering traumatic experiences is an opportunity to incorporate them into the totality of lived experience. Sharing them helps establish community and in that connection we can work creatively, intuitively and compassionately toward alleviating suffering and distress.

PART 1

The Gateway to Practice

DIAGNOSTIC LABELS ACROSS THE LIFE SPAN

Introduction

This chapter reviews psychiatric diagnostic labels and specifically post traumatic stress disorder (PTSD). The diagnostic criteria for PTSD are presented. The process of stigmatisation and psychiatric labelling is discussed along with critical ideas regarding PTSD as a discrete diagnostic category. Some research in relation to PTSD is presented, including neurobiological explanations. The chapter offers a systemic critique of psychiatric diagnostic classifications. Life-cycle issues and the impact of context on behaviours can be used by systemic clinicians in their practice to ensure that diagnostic labels are pragmatically useful.

Psychiatric diagnostic labels

The *Diagnostic and Statistical Manual of Mental Disorders* (DSM) and *International Classification of Diseases* (ICD) provide labels for human behaviours clustered by symptoms that often occur together. It is based on a medical model of illness.

A medical model makes a clear distinction between health and illness. A diagnosis is connected to a treatment plan, a prognosis, and is aimed at returning the individual to a state of health – 'the way things were'.

Psychiatric labels are not 'co-constructed' between client and professional. Co-construction is a process of negotiation between people around the meaning of a communication. Within systemic psychotherapy it is connected to postmodern approaches (Boston, 2000) In postmodern approaches the clinician is not seen as an expert but as a 'conversational partner' (Andersen, 1987).

Within a medical model of diagnostic process, the client and clinician do not consider together the feelings or behaviours that have caused the client to seek help and then agree what these symptoms will be called. A diagnosis is given and sometimes changed with little discussion with or input from the client. Many clients have multiple diagnoses. Children and young people can receive a diagnosis at one stage of their life cycle that carries over into their adult lives, another life-cycle stage.

Receiving a diagnosis can become a passive experience, often followed by an acceptance of the 'agreed' treatment protocol as outlined in the UK by NICE, the **National Institute of Clinical Excellence** (NICE, 2005). These treatment plans are based on research evidence that indicates the intervention which is considered to provide the best relief for the symptoms reported. While this process of diagnosis is more precise in the field of physical health, it is less reliable when it comes to mental health.

Stigmatisation

Mental health diagnoses are often seen as stigmatising. Occasionally some physical health diagnoses are similarly stigmatising – for example HIV/AIDS. Often this stigmatisation is based on fear and ignorance. It can also occur in conjunction with 'either/or' thinking which distinguishes those with mental health problems clearly from those without. Systemic thinking has in the main moved from such dualistic polarities to a more embracing 'both/and' position (Larner, 1994, p 11).

Diagnostic labels are not gender-, class- or race-equitable. This often leads to a minimisation of wider social factors impacting on health. Within mental health, for example, more women than men are diagnosed with depression; more boys than girls are diagnosed with attention deficit hyperactivity disorder (ADHD); black people are over-represented as patients under the **Mental Health Act**. There is no intrinsic reason why these imbalances should exist, which encourages consideration of the wider social contexts impacting on individual functioning. Diagnostic categories are subject to social discourses which systemic clinicians understand as 'clusters of stories including political, economic, and cultural ... personal, family and community...' (Hedges, 2005, p. 3).

The DSM/ICD manuals go through fashions, where diagnoses leave and new ones enter. Take, for example, homosexuality, which was once considered a psychiatric illness. In 1973 the American Psychiatric Association called for removal of homosexuality from the DSM. It was removed and replaced in 1980 with 'ego dystonic homosexuality'. It was not until 1986 that homosexuality as a mental disorder was removed completely from the DSM. Despite its removal, the vestiges of this pathologising of sexual choice can still be coded in the DSM under the category 'Sexual Disorders Not Otherwise Specified' where there is mention of 'persistent and marked disturbance about one's sexual orientation'. These modifications to a diagnosis reflect social and cultural changes about what constitutes a 'mental illness'.

The DSM/ICD diminishes the role of poverty, racism, classism and sexism, all of which link to poor mental health outcomes. This can be seen, for example, with looked-after children, who become 'looked after' because they have suffered **'significant harm'** – a legal term emerging out of UK civil childcare law. Civil courts determine whether the threshold has been reached – has the child suffered or is he or she likely to suffer 'significant harm'? If the answer is 'Yes' the court may decide the child should no longer remain in the care of their family.

'Significant harm' is unequivocally a lived experience caused by variables external to the child. However once a child enters the 'looked-after system', they become subject to a discourse of psychiatric labelling. The rates for 'psychiatric disturbance' in the looked-after children population are considerably higher than for the general population – 45 per cent, a conservative estimate, compared to 10 per cent in the general population (Meltzer *et al.*, 2003; Meltzer, 2005). Yet the obvious discourses about the impact of adverse childhood experiences (often traumatic) on child mental health remain conspicuously absent in the literature. So an extrinsic experience of 'significant harm' becomes an 'intrinsic' experience of 'mental illness'.

Post traumatic stress disorder – the diagnostic category

The diagnostic category post traumatic stress disorder (PTSD) needs to be placed in an historical/hysterical context. Its history reflects wider social factors and lived experiences. The large numbers of men returning from wars showing a typical constellation of behaviours led to the establishment of PTSD as a separate diagnosis. Originally labelled 'shell shock' after the First World War, it was seen as a form of hysteria. With the psychological consequences of further wars (most notably the

Second World War and Vietnam) impacting on generations of families across the globe, PTSD became part of many people's lived experiences.

With increasing globalisation (including media and migration) the impact of war and exposure to other traumatic events has spread far beyond immediate geographical boundaries. This has moved PTSD into common parlance and experience.

PTSD can be reliably diagnosed, often in conjunction with other psychiatric conditions. Not everyone exposed to a risk factor (or the same traumatic experience) develops a PTSD. There is good evidence to suggest that even indirect exposure to traumatic events can generate symptomatic behaviours (Otto *et al.*, 2007), whether this is through media exposure or familial experience. The former (witnessing trauma via the media rather than personally experiencing it) has been dubbed 'post-traumatic stress disorder of the virtual kind' (Young, 2007, p. 21). Research suggests that trauma is very common, with more than half the 'normal' Western population experiencing a traumatic event (Norris and Slone, 2007). Over the life cycle, the chance of experiencing a trauma is put at 69 per cent (Resnick *et al.*, 1993). PTSD is part of a continuum of stress (this is represented in Figure 1.1).

From this large group of people exposed to a traumatic experience (69 per cent), only a small proportion goes on to develop clinically significant PTSD. In North America the figure is between 10 and 20 per cent (Norris and Slone, 2007).

There are a number of factors considered to increase the risk of developing a PTSD. These include the following:

1. Fear at the time of the traumatic experience, particularly a perceived threat to life.
2. Dissociation or a pervasive feeling of detachment from personal experience after the traumatic event.
3. Poor family functioning, including parental mental health problems after the traumatic experience.

(Andrews et al., 2000; Ozer et al., 2003; Trickey, 2009;
Trickey and Black, 2000).

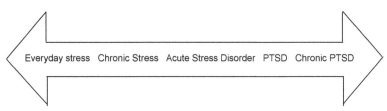

Everyday stress   Chronic Stress   Acute Stress Disorder   PTSD   Chronic PTSD

Figure 1.1   Continuum of Stress

The last factor, poor family functioning after the trauma, emphasises the importance of working with families (and communities) as part of reducing risk and possibly the severity and length of psychological disturbance following traumatic events. For children and young people, it clearly indicates that supporting parents and assessing parental mental health can be essential in promoting the child or young person's recovery. This underlines the usefulness of systemic perspectives in dealing with trauma over the life cycle.

PTSD as a diagnostic category includes delayed onset – allowing for considerable time to pass from the traumatic event to the presentation in a clinical setting. Many clients may not have made a connection between their current somatic experiences and/or emotional distress and earlier traumas.

For example, Jimmy spent much of his childhood in an Irish orphanage where he was subjected to abuse by the staff. In his sixties, he joined with other care survivors to claim compensation for his suffering. He had never been diagnosed with PTSD.

> Your diagnosis of my situation was a great help to me and explained much, of which I had previously been ignorant. With PTSD, there is great after effects and at times seem ongoing through life. I still to this day suffer terrible flashbacks and memories.

In Jimmy's case the diagnosis of PTSD made sense of his lived experience. It also confirmed that his childhood abuse experiences continued to influence his adult life, often in unhelpful ways.

PTSD is seen primarily as an anxiety disorder – with the anxiety having a very distinct quality (Brewin, 2007). There is no secondary processing – no associative representations of the traumatic experience (Verhaeghe, 2004). This is particularly important for systemic clinicians who rely so heavily on narrative interventions which depend on those associative processes.

Much recent discussion about neuropsychology and emotion imply that when the brain's cortex is switched on during conversation, individuals can access words to describe the feeling states that are emerging. However there are times, as in highly stressful, life-threatening situations, when this is not possible. It is not a purposeful switching-off but is automatically triggered by an event (internal felt experience or external stimuli) – an event the individual may not be consciously aware of.

Clinical vignette 1.1 comes from a session where a young girl has been referred to a CAMH service because of her uncontrollable temper.

CLINICAL VIGNETTE 1.1

Speaker	Spoken conversation	Clinical reflections
Mother	It is like this blind rage appears and takes over. (describing her 11-year-old daughter)	'Blind Rage' is the label given for the symptomatic behaviour. This will be tracked through the session. 'Blind Rage' lends itself to **externalizing** because it 'appears and takes over' – the mother sees it as separate to her daughter.
Clinician	Do you know when this is happening? (to daughter)	In checking this out with the daughter consideration is being given to whether she feels has any control and if this is a traumatic enactment.
Daughter	Not really. Just after ... I really need to change my behaviour. (crying)	The response ... 'just after' suggests that during the 'attack' she is dissociated. The crying increases the emotional tone of the session.
Clinician	Do you recognize this blind rage? Is it something you have seen before? (to mother)	Moving back to speak with mother is an attempt to keep the emotional tone manageable and to broaden the discussion out.
Mother	Yes but I don't want to talk about it.	The response suggests a strong affective association for the mother to her daughter's behaviour and avoidance on mother's part to talk about it. This suggests that trauma is very likely a part of the presenting problem.

A history of domestic violence is recorded in the referral. The session is attended by mother and daughter. The child's mother is describing the symptom.Clinical vignette 1.1 is a good description of what may be referred to as an **amygdala hijack** (Goleman, 1996). The girl has little or no awareness about why it happens and when in the grip of one of her rage attacks appears powerless to stop them. When calm, as she was in most of the sessions, she was engaging, cooperative and very sweet. It was hard to imagine what her mother was concerned about. Perhaps the clue comes from mother's comment that the 'blind rage' is something she has seen and/or experienced herself before but doesn't feel able to talk about in the session with her daughter. This shows the multiple layers of experience that need to be worked with in systemic interventions. Not just the here and now of the situation, but also the link to past stories within this family.

This shows how different levels of the system can reverberate across contexts. An amygdala hijack is an example where one brain system (**midbrain**) is privileged over another (the **forebrain**). The midbrain takes over running the 'whole show' rather than working in collaboration – all parts of the brain working together coherently. There are times (contexts) when this hijacking by the midbrain is functional and necessary – where rapid responses in dangerous situations are required for example. However this rapid response can be activated in situations that do not require a rapid response. This can be because the individual who has been traumatised becomes hypervigilant for any danger as well as primed to respond, often referred to as hyperarousal.

In the family system described above, the mother is bringing her daughter to therapy but as the presenting issue is discussed, past issues block the discussion of the present. This makes it hard for mother and daughter to work together to understand what is going on.

DSM criteria

Table 1.1 is the complete DSM criteria for a diagnosis of clinical PTSD. It is provided to help familiarise the reader with the clinical features of PTSD and consider how these may present within clinical settings or during narratives about family life.

The diagnosis of PTSD is often given in conjunction with other psychiatric labels. However, the role of traumatic experiences in the aetiology of many psychiatric/psychological conditions although well documented, can be hidden by the continued use of those other diagnostic categories rather than PTSD. This underlines the importance of understanding the impact of trauma across the life cycle and the need to consider addressing it even when a formal diagnosis of PTSD has not been made.

It is suggested that there are between one to two times as many people who show many of the signs of PTSD, but not all of them (Norris

TABLE 1.1 DSM IV criteria for PTSD

Main criteria	Supporting criteria	Clinical reflections
A. The person has been exposed to a traumatic event in which both of the following were present:	The person experienced, witnessed, or was confronted with an event or events that involved actual or threatened death or serious injury, or a threat to the physical integrity of self or others. The person's response involved intense fear, helplessness, or horror.	This is a subjective definition – the person defines their experience as overwhelming. So for children, they may think they are going to die when in fact this was unlikely. This can also explain a delayed onset where an individual did not think at the time the situation was so dangerous but later recognizes the life-threatening aspect of it. Unless asked about specifically, traumatic events may not come up in sessions.
B. The traumatic event is persistently re-experienced in one (or more) of the following ways:	Recurrent and intrusive distressing recollections of the event, including images, thoughts, or perceptions. Recurrent distressing dreams of the event. Acting or feeling as if the traumatic event were recurring (includes a sense of reliving the experience, illusions, hallucinations, and dissociative flashback episodes, including those that occur on awakening or when intoxicated).	Shame can prevent individuals from disclosing these experiences. Some of the more intense re-experiencing can also not be spoken about as the individual feels 'mad' or 'crazy' and wants to conceal this, especially as the experience feels so real. Sometimes family members give more detailed accounts of symptomatic behaviours.

Main criteria	Supporting criteria	Clinical reflections
	Intense psychological distress at exposure to internal or external cues that symbolize or resemble an aspect of the traumatic event. Physiological reactivity on exposure to internal or external cues that symbolize or resemble an aspect of the traumatic event.	This may be especially true for night terrors and dreams which the individual may not be aware of. This re-experiencing is likely to be present in sessions.
C. Persistent avoidance of stimuli associated with the trauma and numbing of general responsiveness (not present before the trauma), as indicated by three (or more) of the following:	Efforts to avoid thoughts, feelings, or conversations associated with the trauma. Efforts to avoid activities, places, or people that arouse recollections of the trauma. Inability to recall an important aspect of the trauma. Markedly diminished interest or participation in significant activities. Feeling of detachment or estrangement from others. Restricted range of affect (e.g., unable to have loving feelings).	The avoidance of discussing traumatic material can mean many symptomatic behaviours are observed by others. This includes numbed responsiveness, which can be seen as 'normal'. People can forget how they were before the traumatic experience. This avoidance can shape clinical sessions. Clinicians can also avoid discussing what needs to be discussed. It can be experienced as a 'failure to engage'.

Continued

TABLE 1.1   *Continued*

Main criteria	Supporting criteria	Clinical reflections
	Sense of a foreshortened future (e.g., does not expect to have a career, marriage, children, or a normal life span).	
D. Persistent symptoms of increased arousal (not present before the trauma), as indicated by two (or more) of the following:	Difficulty falling or staying asleep. Irritability or outbursts of anger. Difficulty concentrating. Hypervigilance. Exaggerated startle response.	Again if an individual has been suffering for a long time, they may have come to see these symptoms as 'normal' and not recognize how they have changed or been shaped by the experience especially when this involves relational trauma or repeated or chronic exposure to traumatic events. This can make clients very anxious in sessions.
E. Duration of the disturbance (symptoms in Criteria B, C, and D) is more than 1 month.		This underlines the importance of 'time' questions.
F. The disturbance causes clinically significant distress or impairment in social, occupational, or other important areas of functioning.		This is often difficult for an individual to assess especially if PTSD has gone undetected for a considerable period of time. Seeking the observations of significant others such as family or friends can be helpful is ascertaining this.

and Slone, 2007). These people would not be given a diagnosis. Exposure to extreme adverse experiences produces distressed and distressing feelings and behaviours for individuals and families long after the stressors are present in reality. Chronic exposure to trauma can produce changes in personal identity that can lead to stigmatising labels such as borderline personality disorder (BPD), often minimising the role trauma has played in the shaping of the personality.

Systemic perspectives on trauma

Gregory Bateson, considered by many the founder of systemic theory and practice through his work across multiple disciplines, searched for consilience or unity of knowledge. His interest in order and pattern over time has become the scaffold for much of systemic theory.

Bateson in considering a theory of schizophrenia suggested, 'We must not look for some specific traumatic experience [in infantile aetiology] but rather for characteristic sequential patterns [of communication]' (1973, p. 177). He draws attention to the commonly held belief, now supported by much research (see, for example, Schore, 2002), that traumatic experience is shaping. However, he also draws attention to patterns of communication.

This should encourage systemic clinicians to consider the patterns of interaction that follow exposure to traumatic events. By considering the symptoms listed under the diagnostic criteria such as 'avoidance' and 'numbed responsiveness', a systemic clinician can be more sensitive to the communication patterns within sessions where trauma is an issue. 'I don't want to talk about it', will be an all too familiar conversation stopper.

This can then lead to what Bateson termed 'double-bind' communication, where opposing messages at different levels of communicating (for example verbal and nonverbal) are conveyed repetitively and the possibility of addressing this is constrained. In the example given above, the mother has presented her daughter's 'blind rage' as a problem within the family but then feels unable to talk about it.

Many examples of 'double-bind communication' will occur within a systemic clinician's clinical work. Characteristic trauma communication patterns involve 'jumping' from one type of communication to another – from the 'here and now' to 'trauma time'; from one affective state to another quite abruptly; or saying it doesn't matter but showing through body language that it does. Bateson described how 'any part of the double bind sequence may be sufficient to precipitate panic or rage' (Bateson, 1973, p. 179).

Perhaps this is reflecting the process of amygdala hijack. Individuals exposed to such double-bind communication 'cannot, without considerable help, discuss the messages of others. Without being able to do that, the human being is like any self correcting system which has lost its governor; it spirals into never ending but always systematic distortions' (Bateson, 1973, p. 183). A governor is the ability to **meta communicate** and engage in reflexive thought. A traumatic experience (even when it does not result in a diagnosis of PTSD) can rob the individual of that capacity.

Despite what is known about PTSD, there still seems to be a reluctance to diagnose it in certain contexts, such as child and adolescent mental health, along with a huge rise in PTSD diagnoses in other contexts, for example compensation claims. Again this suggests that wider contextual influences are at play.

Critical ideas regarding PTSD

There is much controversy surrounding PTSD. In considering the recent increase in trauma diagnoses, B. Shepherd (quoted in McNally, 2010) was moved to write 'Any unit of classification [PTSD] that simultaneously encompasses the experience of surviving Auschwitz and that of being told rude jokes at work must by any reasonable standard, be a nonsense, a patent absurdity' (McNally, 2010, p. 387; Shepherd, 2004, p. 57).

The word and the diagnosis PTSD appear to have become sanitised. This allows professionals in some instances to avoid considering the horrendous experiences that have led clients to present (Boyle, 2006) and in others to consider unpleasant and difficult emotional experiences as traumatising.

Many systemic clinicians have been critical of using psychiatric labelling as described in the DSM or ICD. Stephen Madigan for example refers to the DSM as 'the professional naming book' (Madigan, 2007, p. 102). It can begin a process of conceptualising mental health as a disease, effectively inhibiting social justice discourses and amplifying discourses around 'born bad' and demonisation (Alon and Omer, 2006).

This focus moves to 'what is wrong with you?' – an identity question – from 'what has happened to you?' – an experience question (Bloom and Farragher, 2011). This reflects an oscillation between two paradoxical processes – maximisation of identity and minimisation of lived experience. This fundamental shift from experience to identity increases the importance given to labelling experience as a mental disorder, including in some cases a 'personality' disorder. This type of labelling can reduce the importance of practical interventions.

Psychiatric labels can become 'identities' in and of themselves. This is reflected in the use of labels to describe a person as their condition for example anorexics, or schizophrenics. This process is not exclusive to psychiatric diagnoses, as many medical conditions can have a similar effect whereby the client becomes their illness – for example asthmatics, diabetics. This would be an example of a 'totalising identity', where an aspect of self or one identity begins to take over other aspects of self or become the dominant identity. This can lead to an acceptance of the identity, and limit attempts to change lived experience.

Clinical vignette 1.2 shows this process unfolding. Chloe (12) is discussing why she is 'in care'. The example shows the use of a psychiatric diagnostic category, paranoid schizophrenia, as an explanation for Chloe's current living arrangements. Chloe has understood certain aspects of the diagnosis, as well as the paradox that her mother's strange ideas had a base in reality. The idea of mental illness is captured in her description of her mother as 'not well'.

The diagnosis appears to be 'totalising' in that Chloe's mother is seen as a 'paranoid schizophrenic' even at times when she is 'well'. Other aspects of her identity such as woman, partner, mother or daughter are not given the same weight as that of paranoid schizophrenic. Because of this, Chloe does not live with her mother, nor is she able to have contact with her mother unsupervised.

While this may be the best course of action at a particular period in time, life-cycle issues are not incorporated into Chloe's care plan. The fluctuating nature of her mother's illness may mean there are times when it is safe enough for Chloe to meet with her. When and how might the situation change over time to allow them to have a different relationship? This underlines the importance of systemic interventions that allow for change over time.

The reification of diagnostic labels draws attention away from traumatic experiences. In considering Chloe's mother's 'paranoid schizophrenia' alongside the description of lived experience from her daughter, we get a glimpse of domestic violence and the hypervigilance it can produce. In the circumstances, the hypervigilance may have been necessary and helpful. It is also clear that a wider conversation is needed with Chloe about her childhood experiences as witness to scenes of violent arguments and threatening behaviour.

When the adverse experiences of adults with mental health problems across a whole range of psychiatric diagnostic categories are examined, a common theme of trauma and abusive childhoods arises (Read *et al.*, 2003).

CLINICAL VIGNETTE 1.2		
Speaker	**Spoken conversation**	**Clinical reflections**
Clinician	Chloe do you know why you are in care?	Exploring the child's under standing of her current context – 'being in care'. Establishing a shared language.
Chloe	Yes it's because my mum is a paranoid schizophrenic.	Child's use of psychiatric term noted – an identity. Child's affect is 'matter of fact'.
Clinician	What does that mean to you Chloe?	Exploring what the term means to the child using curiosity. Co-construction of meaning.
Chloe	She's not well. It's like her brain is split and one part has very strange thoughts and the other part can't control them.	Chloe uses the idea of illness. This raises the issue of how long she thinks she might be in care or a belief when her mother is well she will return home. Chloe's detailed explanation involving the brain – the lack of integration between aspects the brain.
Clinician	Do you remember these strange thoughts – did they show themselves to you?	This curiosity is about how Chloe *experienced* her mother's 'mental illness'.
Chloe	Oh yes she used to sleep with a knife under her pillow because she thought people were trying to get us ... and sometimes people were. George, her boyfriend, used to break the door down and they fought a lot. He also threatened to burn our house down.	This provides material to use in later sessions. It clearly demonstrates how frightening it was for Chloe. In telling this she becomes more animated.

Systemic thinking and diagnostic labels

A systemic approach understands the importance of context and how relationships between individuals or contexts interact to produce understandings or ways of knowing/being. In conversation, meaning emerges and with that aspects of identity (Gergen, 1990, p. 171; Shotter, 1993). In systemic clinical practice, clients are invited to share lived experience and, together with the clinician, reflect on the meanings that arise.

Systemic thinking and practice has distanced itself from a model of individual psychopathology as represented by the DSM and ICD. Yet diagnoses play a pivotal role in accessing mental health services and are likely to do so increasingly as health care becomes more tightly regulated (Berger, 2007). Diagnostic labels are still used in practice and included in many North American systemic training programmes. In part this relates to the healthcare funding, which like compensation cases in the UK, often require a psychiatric diagnosis to be made in order to fund treatment or compensate loss. With changes in healthcare commissioning in the UK, it is likely diagnostic labelling will become increasingly used, despite running contrary to one of the major goals of a systemic approach – to help families understand that the 'problem' is not located in the individual but arises in a context. Diagnoses are likely to remain as organising concepts in treatment, interwoven as they are with NICE guidelines (Roth and Fonagy, 2004).

A PTSD diagnosis may increase the chances of psychotherapy being offered as opposed to medication alone. It can change how a situation that seemed inexplicable can be understood differently – offering a different lens. In the past, systemic therapies frequently understood the child as the symptom-bearer for the parents'/family's dysfunction (see, for example, Byng-Hall, 1980). The field has moved away from using such language (symptom-bearer) and works towards promoting an understanding that the 'problem' exists relationally and as a consequence is best worked with relationally.

Personal parlance and medical jargon represent a clash of dialects (Barbaro et al., 2008). By adopting the language of psychiatry, one can end up denying one's own experience/identity. In 1973 David Rosenhan conducted what is now seen as a classic study: 'Being Sane in Insane Places'. It looked at the way context affects how individuals are perceived, and challenged psychiatric diagnostic labels by asking participants to fake a psychiatric condition. The pseudo-patients were all admitted and diagnosed with psychiatric conditions, most frequently schizophrenia. Once admitted they then behaved normally. Their admissions ranged from seven to 52 days.

Similarly the Zimbardo prison study demonstrated 'what happens when you put good people in an evil place' (Haney, Banks and Zimbardo, 1973) This involved randomly allocating male students to roles of either prisoner or prison guard in a mock prison setting and assessing their behaviours once in role. The study was intended to last seven to 14 days but stopped abruptly after only six.

More recently Richard Bentall (2009) offers an anecdote that suggests these findings about roles and context from decades ago remain just as relevant today:

> Puzzled by the lack of any psychotic behaviour, [RB] asked the ward staff how a client was settling in following an admission 'He's excessively polite'. 'Can you be excessively polite?' he wondered ... 'We're trying to work out whether his politeness is part of his normal personality or his illness'.

This suggests identities and the meaning of communications are determined by context.

Barbaro and colleagues (2008) found that clients admitted to psychiatric hospital were deemed to be 'getting better' as they began to describe their experiences using psychiatric language rather than their own. An example given as 'I talk to God' (personal explanation) versus 'I suffer auditory hallucinations' (professional explanation). A diagnosis can 'oblige [you] to bring your individual experience into line with "official dogma" the version of reality endorsed by the rest of the world' (Barbaro *et al.*, 2008). How can a context be created for individual, linguistically defined versions of the experienced world to manifest? (Rostworowska *et al.*, 2005).

Moving through the life cycle, adverse childhood experiences and traumatic experiences can become more invisible as labels or care pathways takeover and become defining of identity.

Transgenerational transmission

The trauma literature also raises the idea of transgenerational transmission. If a parent cannot regulate their own affect autonomously, how will they be able to help their children do so?

This can then become an indirect exposure to trauma for the child to their parent's traumatic experience. While other psychiatric diagnoses also show a link between generations, this is most often described through a discourse of genetics rather than experiential exposure.

In exploring this concept of transgenerational transmission, it has been found, for example, that children of Holocaust survivors run a higher risk of developing PTSD than others (Yehuda *et al.*, 1998a, b). This idea is captured in the film 'Waltz with Bashir' (Folman, 2008), where the protagonist (Ari) is searching to fill gaps in his memory about his own war experiences in the Lebanon. In this segment he is talking to a friend (Carmi Cna'an):

> your interest in the massacre developed a long time before it happened ... [it] stems from another massacre ... [it] is actually the 'other' camps. Were your parents in camps?

This explanation of transgenerational transmission is also captured in the Peruvian film *La Teta Asustada* [*The Milk of Sorrow*, 2009]. Fausta, the film's protagonist is taken to a hospital by her uncle after a fainting fit. Fausta's uncle gives the doctor his explanation for his niece's condition:

> Fausta was born during terrorism and her mother transmitted her fear through her breast milk. The milk of sorrow as we call anyone born that way without a soul because it hid underground out of fear.

The idea of being so frightened that the soul hides away often occurs in trauma narratives. This moves into other more spiritual discourses far removed from psychiatric understandings. However, finding and joining with clients in the explanations that speak to them is an essential part of systemic practice. This represents the co-creation of stories that help produce change and transformation.

The research supports Fausta's uncle's explanation. Often children whose parents have been traumatised, display more PTSD disturbance than their parents (Yehuda *et al.*, 1998a, b) without having been exposed to any apparent traumatic stressor. The hypervigilance and hyperarousal associated with traumatic responses, sensitises the family system and puts children at increased risk of developing a PTSD if they do experience a traumatic event.

Parents primarily provide the child with the language through which the world can be experienced and any trauma processed (Smith, 2005b, 2008). This is reflected in the findings of Andrews *et al.* (2000) who listed parental psychological functioning post traumatic experience as a significant factor in the aetiology of and recovery from PTSD. For many parents, the natural response is to not discuss disturbing material with children. So while a parent may provide language to describe a range of experiences for their child, it is commonly believed that not talking about trauma is the best way forward.

The following example comes from clinical practice. Kate is looking after her grandchild following the murder of her daughter-in-law by her son. The current clinical issue revolved around telling her grandchild about how 'mummy' had died. Transgenerational ideas of domestic violence are explored and how stories about it can emerge.

> Kate had lived with a domestically violent husband who manifested pathological jealously and frequently threw her out of the house. His psychological violence increased throughout her brief marriage. Like many women in domestically violent relationships, she thought she kept it hidden from her son. One peak episode involved her being thrown out of the family home by her husband. She described being unable to get her 5-year-old son out. She could still see him at the top of the stairs looking at her. This image of shared helplessness is some-thing she recalled clearly. This is likely to be a traumatic flashback. She enlisted the help of her sisters who lived down the road. Kate went back to get her son. She and her son never returned to the family home again, but they also never discussed what happened. This avoidance is a typical feature of traumatic experience.

Themes from her own experience of domestic violence (in particular pathological jealousy) manifested in the lives of the next generation. Once Kate had left Omar's father, these themes were no longer physi-cally present in Omar's childhood or early adolescence. Yet their 'psychic presence' remained.

This shows how life-cycle transitions can activate material from past traumatic events. When Omar became a young man and began having intimate relationships, he found it hard to trust his partner. He began to ruminate on her leaving him. In trying to think of how to talk with her grandchild, Kate realised she never talked about the domestic violence or pathological jealousy she experienced with her son. She actively avoided discussing it. She had convinced herself this was the best thing to do.

Not talking about critical issues at one stage of development may be appropriate but necessary at another. This formed part of our discus-sion. What was an age-appropriate explanation for her grandchild and how will it need to be modified in light of his increasing understanding over time and his own progress through life-cycle stages.

This does not mean to imply that had Kate discussed the domestic violence and pathological jealousy Omar witnessed and lived with in the early years of his childhood, the tragic outcome would have been prevented. But it became clear that this untold story was still full of palpable raw unprocessed emotion. It suggested that Kate was still traumatised by her experience of domestic violence. It also suggested that perhaps Omar had also been traumatised by his experience of living with domestic violence. The repetitions of themes such as 'pathological jealousy' underline the power of stories over generations and how they can shape behaviours even when not spoken about. It may be that in discussing such issues, these patterns of behaviour are less likely to repeat.

Mentalisation and trauma

Talking about trauma can help if it activates the capacity to mentalise and reflect. **Mentalisation**, the act of interpreting the actions of oneself and others, and reflective functioning fail to develop for those traumatised chronically in early childhood (Fonagy and Target, 1996; Schore, 2003a, b).

For adults traumatised in later life when mentalisation and reflective functioning have developed; reminders of the traumatic experience act as triggers to switching off these processes. In the grip of a traumatic flashback, the capacity to imagine what others are feeling or to make sense of what you are feeling is lost. The narrative functions of lived experience are seriously compromised. This compromise can be intermittent. This is significant for systemic psychotherapists whose treatment interventions are so strongly mediated by language, narrative and capacity to reflect. Without mentalisation, talking can become a reliving or re-enactment.

Deprived of narrative, trauma will be encoded or remembered primarily as a somatic experience. 'Lacking the possibility of being psychologically processed, the trauma is inscribed on the body itself' (Van der Kolk, 1994; Verhaeghe, 2004, p. 316). Systemic therapy's relationship to the body remains undeveloped despite its theoretical understanding of systems and the interaction between them – including mind–body (Bertrando and Gilli, 2008).

Neurobiological ideas

The emerging research on neurobiology confirms unequivocally that 'our brains ... are constructed by interactions with other' (Siegel, 1999;

Soloman and Siegel, 2003). Nature and nurture are mutually recursive (Fishbane, 2007). As experience alters the brain, there is reason to believe that change is possible over the life course. However habitual the neural pathways may be, new experiences can generate new neural pathways. Trauma blocks out 'news of difference' – diminishing the effects of trauma on lived, thinking and feeling experience is essential so that new habitual neural pathways can be generated.

Interactions with caregivers allow the child's brain to develop the neural structures necessary to move from dyadic regulation to more autonomous forms of self regulation (Siegel and Hartzell, p. 215 quoted in Fishbane 2007). During the acquisition phase of life (early childhood and adolescence) under optimum conditions, self regulation of emotion and development of a range of responses to any given situation including stressful ones through relationship are key tasks.

If an individual is chronically stressed and traumatised by early experiences they are likely to have poor self regulation of emotion; increased stress responses which compromise immune functioning and disrupt social functioning (*Foresight Mental Capital and Wellbeing Project*, 2008) – a vicious cycle. Good enough relational experience produces a 'feels felt' experience (Siegel and Hartzell, 2003). This allows an individual to move away from stress responses to new experience. It promotes a sense of well being, which in turn promotes immune functioning that maintains physical health – a virtuous cycle.

Life-cycle issues

Diagnostically, it may be more helpful from a systemic perspective to see the individual in a context of endless shifting meanings embedded within a larger linguistic sociocultural context, in which symptoms become signifiers rather than signs of distress (Verhaeghe, 2004). This allows for life-cycle transitions and changes to the meaning of past experiences to emerge.

Angela, a Care System Survivor, is reflecting on experiences many decades earlier:

> I have a lot of anger regarding my childhood years. I know my foster mother was good to me but I have in later years found myself putting some blame on her for allowing them to take me away from her. I also feel angry she didn't tell me more about my background.

Her understanding of her situation has changed over time, often influenced by her own life-cycle issues. She had been placed in foster care from a young age and then removed to an institution from her foster family. Initially all she could think of was her foster family but as the decades have passed, she now wondered about her birth family more than she had done previously.

Symptoms can be seen as metaphorical signposts working towards understanding the individual in a specific context. In this way symptomatic behaviours are **reframed** as helpful in providing a direction to discussions, conversations and stories about healing. It helps to underline the fluidity of identity and the importance of lived experience.

Memory takes us where we need to go. (Carmi Cna'an in Folman, 2008.)

Diagnostic labels and context

A psychiatric labelling system may seem to be a convenient way to understand experience and to make sense of it. Victor Frankl (2011) in his logotherapy outlined the importance of meaning making when suffering is experienced.

Suffering can cause relational paradigm shifts – to see oneself and others in a different light. Consider 'Stockholm syndrome', where the adverse but intimate forced relationship resulted in a common understanding by the captives of the captor. Or the less well known 'Lima syndrome' where the captors became so sympathetic towards their captives, they let them all go.

Understanding of self relates to the meanings given to lived experiences and in turn these meanings shape identity. Meaning arises relationally. Individually and collectively identities are constructed over time, then accessed in a variety of ever-changing contexts (Gergen, 2009). Identity and, perhaps more accurately, identities are not static but dynamic and recreated through relational experiences.

By arriving at an agreed definition of what needs to be worked on – which may include an understanding of how the problem has come to be – it becomes possible to begin to generate a range of solutions within the skills set and knowledge of the helping system. The relational context of a therapeutic experience allows a client to consider who they have been, are now, want to be in the future, and how these identities manifest in lived experience.

While a diagnostic label may describe a particular state, it is important to remain connected to the range of possible consequences, not just negatives ones, that arise from traumatic experience. Clinicians need to consider how life-cycle transitions may impact on the meaning and understanding of a particular experience.

A diagnostic label is but one story amongst many embedded in the multiple contexts of lived experience – with each story being privileged within a specific context. By taking a life-cycle perspective a process of recognition begins that can be elaborated and developed over time without becoming the totality of the individual's identity. In therapy this produces an opening up of 'an alternative territory of identity' (White, 2005a). An understanding based on individual pathology is only one tiny part of the meaning making matrix of life which includes family, community and wider sociopolitical/spiritual contexts.

Conclusion

Systemic therapists can 'establish contexts in which people can give full voice to their experiences of trauma' (White, 2005a). The DSM/ICD may help to regard at a distance the pain of others (Sontag, 2003). Clinicians need to avoid a process whereby violence turns anybody subjected to it into a thing (Weil, 1940). This is especially pertinent for trauma experiences. The reification of psychiatric labels can become another form of violence – a psychological violence by colonising (Fredman, 2004; Rober and Seltzer, 2010) someone's emotional and physical experiences. It can become silencing of untold stories.

Systemic approaches allow for a freedom of movement between contexts, extracting what is needed in each context to allow the 'heart, mind and spirit' to remain at the forefront of mental health interventions, whilst also giving traumatic experiences attention and respect. This focus on multiple contexts helps to develop and maintain the psychological resilience that enables clients to live with and through a traumatic experience.

2

Resiliencies Across the Life Span

Introduction

This chapter will focus on the theoretical concept of psychological resilience. Characteristics traditionally associated with resilience will be outlined and summarised. This is intended to help systemic therapists incorporate more specifically narratives of resilience in their work. Traumatic experiences can overwhelm resilient responses. Cultivating and nurturing these 'exceptions' to the numbed responsiveness of trauma must be a key component of therapeutic experience.

Theoretical overview

Resilience as a concept needs a postmodern reconstruction. It needs to be considered as a co-constructed emergent quality, rather than one which resides somewhere within an individual. Cronen and Pearce (1980) discuss the hierarchy of contexts in their seminal paper on the **'coordinated management of meaning'** (**CMM**). This model sees communication as constitutive, and examines patterns of interaction considering a variety of contexts and particularly the highest context at a given time. This means an experience can be perceived from an individual point of view at one time and at a different time from a wider political perspective; for example. CMM has evolved since its original formulation and is now applied to consider moving towards a 'higher order of relational consciousness' (Pearce, 2007).

Taking this approach of multiple contexts simultaneously present at any one time for any one action, it can be useful to think of resilience not as singular but plural. Resiliencies are relational processes emerging through meaning created between different multiple contexts. This represents potentially multiple layers of resilience where recovery from traumatic events is more likely. Resiliencies are socially constructed and relationally enacted (Smith, 1999).

Considering a hierarchy of levels, starting at the individual felt experience, a traumatic event impacts on an individual's neurobiology, the individual sense of self, the immediate context and the context's context. Meaning or making sense of the traumatic experience will be generated through the interplay of each of these levels. For example, the felt experience of rape (clearly a traumatic event) may be disproved in court through a not guilty verdict (a socio/political context). This dissonance between levels of experience is likely to produce distress and confusion in making sense of personal experience.

Resilience is multifactorial, it changes over time, and is different for different people. It extends from clearly genetic predispositions, such as temperament and intelligence, to contextual, as in family or community variables. It includes broad themes such as humour, spirituality and 'outlook on life'. Considering the multiple contexts impacting on the individual lived experience provides for a range of combinations and permutations in relation to resilient outcomes. This helps avoid belief systems, which could construe poor outcomes as solely related to individual deficits, rather than failures at many levels from the neurobiological, individual, family, social and political. It helps to focus attention on contexts that promote healing and growth despite adversity.

Experiencing a traumatic event or accumulating a number of adverse childhood experiences increases the risk for poor health outcomes (Felitti *et al.*, 1998). The risk can only be reduced by increasing health-maximizing behaviours. In clinical work this means building on resiliencies in the widest sense (Gorell Barnes, 1999; Rutter, 1999; Smith, 1999).

A trauma-based world-view changes the way safety and predictability of relationships are experienced. It becomes constrictive, restrictive and periodically explosive. A resilience-based world-view draws on beliefs about managing hardships; getting through difficult times. It promotes a sense of self efficacy through relationships. In contrast to a trauma-based world-view, it is expressive, fluid and periodically transcendent.

As Elsa Jones (2007, p. 150) notes: 'Moving on ... entails no longer being confined by a survivor identity but being free to construct a life that has meaning beyond the past and its overwhelming definition of self as someone who is circumscribed by the experience'.

Vulnerabilities and resiliencies are not stand-alone components but aspects that go into the totality of the living web of connections, where the whole is much greater than the sum of its parts. Individuals can be both vulnerable and resilient simultaneously, depending on the context. They are not anchors of a single polarity but two separate strands intersecting across the life cycle through time and experience. At certain transition points they may seem very closely aligned and intricately connected – so it can be easy to move between them. This intertwining is fundamentally important, as it offers multiple opportunities to reclaim, resume, re-examine and reinstate health. It helps to shift systemic therapies to a pragmatic focus of utility, rather than a search for truth (Barge, 2004, p. 196).

Trauma and resilience are 'imbricated' – overlapping in regular patterns over the life cycle (Varela, 1979). They represent two different discourses but emerge from the relationship with the other. One's resilience emerges in response to overwhelming stress and one's experience of trauma overwhelms one's resilience. Resilience is a product of close collaboration and mutual co-construction between multiple systems – self, family and community – it is emergent. The meaning-making systems that surround these aspects of self determine the dominant narrative.

Trauma as a crucible for resilient identities

Sometimes a traumatic experience is said to 'bring out the best' in people. In the face of extreme adversity, individuals can sometimes develop an aspect of self and elevate it to heroic proportions.

Sandor Ferenczi wrote about the possibility that trauma can promote development in 1933. He described:

> ... the sudden, surprising rise of new faculties after a trauma, ... Great need, and more especially mortal anxiety seem to possess the power to waken up suddenly and to put into operation latent dispositions ... One is justified – in contradistinction to the familiar regression – to speak of a traumatic progression of a precocious maturity (Ferenczi in Borossa, 1999, p. 301).

The phrase 'put into operation latent dispositions' underlines the idea that resilient identities are always present but not necessarily evident.

More recently Papadopoulos has used the phrase 'adversity activated development' which includes positive developments which have resulted from experiences gained after/during exposure to adversity/trauma (Papadopoulos, 2007).

Traumatic experience can compromise the ability to process and modulate the emotional aspects of experience (Schore, 2003a, b). This 'emotional numbness' will be amplified if the immediate significant network and wider social context also find it difficult to tolerate and manage the feelings caused by the event. Traumatised individuals have greater need of the 'other' to help them through the traumatic experience – whether this is parent, partner, significant other or clinician. Resilience for any one experience may reside in 'other' for a period of time. In the absence of safe, secure relationships it can be difficult to confront traumatic experience.

Like other traumatic event research, such as loss of a parent in childhood (Bifulco *et al.*, 1992), it may be that the event in and of itself does not necessarily produce negative long-term outcomes. It is more likely to do so if the sequelae to the event leads to other negative experiences, such as reception into care, and/or the experience fundamentally affects the view of self and how self may be viewed by others.

The following sections examine levels of context through a lens of systemic practice.

Individual neurobiological context

Systemic practitioners do not need to abandon ideas about the brain, or body, and how experience impacts at the physical level. Consider for example how early systemic ideas arose from the study of biological systems by Ludwig Von Bertalanfy (1968) and his 'general systems theory', or the work of Humberto Maturana and Francisco Varela regarding the 'theory of autopoiesis' about the nature of reflexive feedback in living systems. Other systemic practitioners clearly consider and are curious about the interaction between body and mind, for example Bateson (1973), Harré (1997) and Bertrando and Gilli (2008).

Maturana and Varela (1980, p. 13) saw living systems as 'cognitive systems, and living as a process of cognition. This statement [was considered] valid for all organisms, with or without a nervous system'.

Varela was a proponent of embodied philosophy which argued that our thoughts, beliefs and consciousness can only be understood in terms of the enactive structures in which they arise, namely the body (understood both as a biological system and as personally, phenomenologically experienced) and the physical world with which the body interacts. He called this study **neurophenomenology**. These ideas about systems migrated across to the field of human communications.

Some life stories may remain linguistically incoherent. This may relate to early childhood trauma before language developed. When traumatic experiences have no words, memories can be held in the body (Levine, 1997; Ogden *et al.*, 2006; Rothschild, 2000; Van der Kolk, 1994). Even when traumatic experience is worded, it can remain held in the body. Increasingly there is a move to work systemically in a more integrated way, incorporating many different modalities into the recovery process not just worded interventions (Denborough, 2008; Wilson, 2007).

This example of a newborn baby, acts as a reminder that infants also experience mental health and are affected by exposure to stress. Rachelle was referred to a CAMH Service as part of assessing her long term care plan.

Rachelle was born 10 weeks premature to a mother who had experienced domestic violence during her pregnancy. Both of these experiences constitute stressors. Rachelle remained in a special care baby unit (SCBU) for her first six weeks before being placed with her foster mother. SCBUs are often quite stressful noisy environments, with bright lights and the absence of long periods of nurturing touch. While in the SCBU her mother visited only intermittently. Her foster mother describes Rachelle crying while asleep; showing hyperarousal and startle responses to loud noises and bright lights; tense and rigid body following contact with her mother, coupled with irritability and an inability to settle without much cosseting.

We could language Rachelle's experience. We know that the infant's brain is experience dependent and that the primary caregiver (usually mother) co-creates the child's internal sense of emotional security (Schore, 2003a, b). In this example Rachelle is already primed neurochemically for anxious responses through her prenatal and perinatal experiences.

Her contact programme with her biological mother, pending the outcome of care proceedings, keeps her sensitised to distress. It is delivered in an adult-focused way, with no attention being paid to the emotional wellbeing of a baby. Different adults come to the foster carer's home to take Rachelle to see her biological mother three times per week. Her foster carer is helping to co-create Rachelle's internal sense of emotional security against a backdrop of agitation and irritability and with regular separations or stressors to their relationship.

This story of her early months can be easily lost as Rachelle moves through the 'care system', especially as she is considered too young to remember. However it is likely this traumatic start to life will be remembered bodily.

Neuropsychological research suggests that Rachelle's experience-dependent brain will develop a low immune system setting and a high neuroendocrine response. She will be easily stressed. This neurological understanding becomes another layer of meaning to consider.

Consilience is occurring – a congruence of meaning across disciplines. We are hard wired for what Daniel Siegel (1999) calls 'mindsight', the ability of the mind to see itself, but this ability needs to be nurtured and shaped through experience. Traumatic experiences can cause toxic ruptures (Siegel and Hartzell, 2003, p. 193) to our relationships across many levels. Rachelle has already experienced 'toxic ruptures'.

Rachelle's current primary caregiver can act as an affect regulator for her, but Rachelle lives in a wider context that does not privilege this relationship or its reparative effects for her adverse start to life. Rachelle is moved to another placement at a critical stage when she is showing selective attachment behaviours to her primary caregiver. This further separation is another trauma for Rachelle given the timing. It was done abruptly, not gradually, based on the idea that Rachelle will not remember this stage of her life. However, it is extremely likely this lived experience will be remembered. This demonstrates how one context (social care and legal proceedings) can be privileged over another (child's developmental stage) despite the intention to work in the child's best interest. This often arises because of incompatible and incongruent time frames.

While talking therapies try to make sense of traumatic experiences through the development of coherent narratives of experience, it appears more specific attention needs to be paid to building a repertoire of self-soothing techniques. Mindfulness and yoga are two examples of interventions aimed at integrating mind and body now being used in trauma work (Dimeff and Linehan, 2001; Emerson and Hopper, 2011; Briere interviewed by Goldstein, 2010; Kabat-Zinn, 1991; Van der Kolk, 2009). These will directly contribute to the individual neurobiological connections that promote wellbeing.

In therapy Margo described how her 'higher self' was waking her up at 5 a.m. every morning for meditation. A friend had suggested it was really her 'anxiety' that was waking her. Margo described thinking on this and deciding she preferred the idea that her 'higher self' was orchestrating these early morning calls. Neurologically this is the time when the **pineal body** hands over control to the **pituitary gland**. It is also considered a good time for spiritual practice. Choosing to believe in her 'higher self' rather than her 'anxiety' as setting the tone for the day is an example of privileging resilience. The clinician can support the resilient narrative of 'higher self' over the pathologising narrative of 'anxiety'.

The above example highlights both an intervention aimed at the neurobiological level – practicing meditation at a certain time of the day to influence the production of neurotransmitters – and how the individual belief system supports the practice. This is an example where beliefs confirm actions and help to develop a coherent approach to managing a stressful situation. The articulation of this becomes a narrative.

The current emphasis on the individual aspects of resilience minimises wider social factors that have increased stressors for the individual and generated more complex information to process. The ever-increasing overload of information often encourages individuals to be more active. Rather than spending time on 'quietening the mind', information over load is often managed through stimulants and drugs, including alcohol, caffeine and nicotine. This escalation can lead to 'burn out'.

In considering exposure to trauma, agitation and anxiety often over-whelm individuals. They can become involved in doing too much and find inaction to be uncomfortable because when the mind is allowed to lose the focus on action, unwanted intrusive memories surface that the activity was keeping at bay.

This example comes from a self-soothing programme run for kinship carers (Smith and Lewis). The programme combines teaching and experiential components around different sense experiences, including breath control, visualisations, sound, smell, touch and physical activity. At the end of each session is a brief period of guided relaxation.

This was Afia's first time attending the group. Afia is seeking asylum in the UK. As the relaxation began, by focusing on the breath, Afia became agitated and afraid. When talking to her, it became clear that speaking in English, not her first language, and living in England kept her traumatic memories away. Being asked to be quiet, and rest in silence with others she didn't know very well, filled her head with unwanted memories. Afia felt she couldn't relax and had to keep busy all the time. When she stopped she often found she became profoundly depressed, unable to move or do anything. This oscillation between extremes was part of avoiding talking and thinking about what she had survived.

Resilience and individual beliefs

Traumatic experience can have a negative effect on an individual's sense of themselves. Traumatic experiences can lead to actual physical damage, but even in the absence of this the sense of being damaged is often central. **Reframing** the sense of being damaged to one of being changed can start to develop narratives of hope and resilience.

The personal meaning of traumatic experience will determine whether resilience or trauma shape future narratives. If the socially ascribed meaning is also one which construes 'self' as fundamentally ruined (as is often the case in relational trauma) this can have very damaging consequences especially if 'self' is viewed as a unitary abiding concept.

Aoife was asked to keep a journal during therapy and write down any thoughts or ideas she had following sessions. She was asked to consider some of the ideas she grew up with about women. Her daughter has been sexually abused by a trusted adult who befriended her family. Aoife felt a failure as a mother. It has also activated her own experiences of sexual abuse as a child. This was making it hard for her to be the parent she wanted to be for her daughter. She wrote:

> Be strong. Women must be strong in the face of adversity; in the face of men's bullying passive aggressive tactics (no more mr nice guy). Children must be protected by any means possible.

She is reflecting on the contradictory messages she received to be 'nice' but also strong and how this contradiction made it difficult for her to confront the man who was sexually abusing her daughter. This made her feel a failure because she felt she did not protect her daughter when she had grown up with a strongly held belief that children must be protected.

Traumatic experiences can narrow perceptual awareness to that which is necessary for survival. In the healing process this often needs to be said – the reminder of the overwhelming nature of trauma where not all aspects of self were available. Aoife's own experience of sexual abuse as a child made it hard for her to be the mother she wanted to be – the mother she never had.

If traumatic experience is not processed it can be relived or re-enacted, with the possibility for new learning reduced. One's ability to see different aspects of self can also be compromised to a dominant view defined by the traumatic experience, possibly as victim or survivor. Only survival continues as opposed to living. Keeping a wider perspective and encouraging Aoife to move between layers of her experience as a child, a woman and a mother helped to keep her in her role as parent and protector for her daughter. Supporting her daughter through therapy was protective. Reminding her that her daughter had told her about her experiences and that she had believed her daughter without hesitation, taking immediate steps to protect her and find help for her, despite no criminal prosecution being brought, helped to strengthen her story of herself as a protective parent and diminish her catastrophic story of parental failure.

Both the meaning ascribed to experiences and those that are ascribed by others, have the greatest impact on how stories of self are managed. In therapy, Aoife moved from feeling helpless to finding inner resources to cope. She could see how the trusted adult had made her feel she could entrust the care of her daughter to him without raising her suspicions and how, when she was suspicious, he had convinced her she was remembering her own experiences rather than accurately assessing the current situation.

Secret shameful identities

A 'frozen narrative' could be described as 'numbed responsiveness', representing the 'foreshortened sense of the future' outlined in the diagnostic framework of PTSD in Chapter 1. Trauma can disable the ongoing process of identity, stunting or freezing it to one time and one place. Traumatic experiences and identities can become the dominant and shaping aspect of self. Angela describes herself as a 'detainee' when considering her experiences in care in the late 1950s.

Considering it was for a short time, it's had an enormous impact on my life. I have learnt from my records the reason given for detainment. 'Having a parent who does not exercise proper guardianship'. In other words she was a bad mother. How that pains me. I am now beginning to understand how we could never talk about what happened. I spent years thinking I had let her down, and I never wanted her to know how much pain I had gone through in those short few years away from her as it would have made her unhappy. I am so glad I never told her as I feel she was punished enough. ... A detainee 1958–1961.

The descriptor 'detainee' highlights the pejorative label given to a child taken into care in Ireland more than fifty years ago. Angela often returned to this label, wondering what it was she had done to deserve such a punishment. The label still holds psychological resonance for her – but not all of the time, only in certain contexts. At those times, the repertoire of self becomes limited and the more resilient aspects of Angela's identity less visible. This example also shows how secrets can sometimes have a protective effect.

Secrets often serve a protective function – allowing aspects of self to be preserved which full disclosure strips away. The move in systemic psychotherapy away from models of truth to a more dialogical approach recognises that different contexts allow different identities to emerge. Something can be secret in one context but known about in another.

Using journals in therapy can help clients bring previously 'untold, untellable, unheard, unknown stories' into the therapeutic space and allow more complex and expanded narratives of self to emerge (Kearney, 2004). Pete was asked to write about 'confronting your fears' as part of an inter-session reflection. Pete had a history of childhood abuse, including extreme physical violence. This is an excerpt from his journal:

> I just want oblivion. I want out of this life. I really do. I can't make the pain stop. I am frightened to be around small children because I have fleeting images of hurting them. I am so very frightened and disgusted admitting that. I will never act upon these feelings.

In the excerpt, a number of important issues arise that had not previously been spoken about in therapy. The journal was written to be read. This begins to open it up as a form of relational communication. In therapy, focusing on the construction 'this life' allowed discussion about what other lives Pete may want for himself.

Pete was asked to consider if the 'fleeting images' were connected to any specific feelings and whether these images might be traumatic flashbacks to his own experience. Pete talked about the images arising when he felt anger. Thinking about the images as flashbacks to his own experience helped Pete to feel compassion for himself as a child and responsible for himself as an adult. It strengthened his determination to 'never act on these feelings'. This conflation of time, where adult self experiences child self, can be very disturbing. Considering the images as flashbacks to his own traumatic childhood encouraged Pete to discuss his childhood experiences in more detail. He had not previously done so. He had developed strategies to cope with his feelings and tried to avoid situations that triggered memories for him. He had also decided he could never be a parent.

Shameful aspects of experience and identity often fall into the untold, untellable part of narrative work. This often leads to people being in conversation with self. However, it is difficult to introduce alternative reparative voices. 'Clients seek more than the liberation of their own subjugated knowledge' (Pare quoted in Rober, 2005). This experience of difference arises in the dialectic between one aspect of self and other (Verhaeghe, 2004). Systemic interventions can bridge the gap between stories of overwhelming trauma and resilience, mindful that both these aspects of identity arise relationally. In sharing his fear of hurting small children, Pete was able to change his own point of view, to see himself as a small child once and now as a protector of children. This was in stark contrast to the secret fear of being a potential perpetrator of violence on children.

Spirituality

Narratives of resilience can become transformative, especially when attention to more spiritual aspects of identity are addressed. I have worked with a large number of adults abused in the care system by religious people entrusted with their upbringing. This has led to discussions about the impact this has had on their spiritual practice. Jimmy shared this extract from a letter he wrote to the *Sunday Independent* on 16 November 2003. It demonstrates many aspects of resilience and shows how it coexists with traumatic experiences.

> I have my own religion – it is nature. I talk to God through the trees, shrubs and flowers that I cultivate. I now work at a care and residential home for the elderly folks. I enjoy bringing a smile to their faces. ... I love my job and it helps to take my mind off my problems. ... The Catholic religion was well and truly KICKED OUT OF ME. But I still have my spiritual beliefs and do it my way through helping the old and my gardening and love of animals.

Jimmy and I discussed how he had taken up work in a care facility – one which offered a truly caring environment for its residents and that he contributed to creating that 'caring' environment. This seemed to be a form of reparation.

He had devised a personal spiritual practice. So rather than relinquishing the manifestation of mystery in day-to-day life because of his abuse within a religious context, he has embraced this mystery in his own way, recognising its sustaining power.

In 2008, the New Economics Foundation (NEF) was commissioned by the UK government's **Foresight project** on Mental Capital and Wellbeing to review the interdisciplinary work of scientists from across the world and identify a set of evidence-based actions to improve wellbeing. These have been condensed and summarised as 'five ways to wellbeing'. They are: 'Connect', 'Be active', 'Take Notice', 'Keep Learning' and 'Give'. Jimmy's excerpt shows all of these in practice. By writing he is making a connection with others. His work keeps him active and connected. His love of nature means he takes notice of his environment. His love of animals and gardening are new areas of learning. His care taking at the facility is an example of giving.

This shows his resilience, despite his traumatic experiences. Yet for years he had no idea that his quality of life had been severely compromised by his care experiences, or that the difficulties he had experienced with flashbacks, periods of depression and problems in his personal relationships could be connected to what had happened to him when in care. Like Angela, he had grown up with a sense of worthlessness and shame. He felt responsible for what had happened to him, and for many years the wider systems of state and church denied his lived experience.

Family stories of resilience

Traumatic experience does not just affect the individual who has experienced it. Anyone who has lived with someone who has been traumatised, for example foster parents of children who have been severely abused, or children of war survivors, can sometimes see and feel the effects more clearly than the individual themselves (see, for example, Cairns, 2010).

The impact of trauma and family relationships was captured in the *Commission to Inquire into Child Abuse Report* (CICA) (2009), also known as the Ryan Report, commissioned by the Irish Government to investigate the widespread abuse of children in Irish care facilities from 1936 onwards. The report noted in its executive summary:

> The enduring impact of childhood abuse was described by many witnesses who, while reporting that as adults they enjoyed good relationships and successful careers, had learned to live with their traumatic memories. Many other witnesses reported that their adult lives were blighted by childhood memories of fear and abuse. They gave accounts of troubled relationships and loss of contact with their siblings and extended families (p. 14).

I interviewed many adults, including sibling groups, who had all been in institutions where abuse had been endemic, including the orphanages in Ireland and the approved schools in north-west England and

Wales. For many, the multiple abuse experiences within the care system were kept secret from their parents, partners and other members of the family. It was not until the police became involved in large retrospective investigations that this secret aspect of their lived experience became public. This was not always to good effect. In part this previous secrecy was sometimes seen as a means of protecting others (often parents and partners) or concealing aspects of identity they felt unable 'to live with'. This serves as a reminder that secrecy is not always negative and can serve as the gatekeeper of sacred experience (Bateson and Bateson, 1987).

The disclosure that the 'care' offered by the state/church involved emotional abuse, neglect, physical brutalisation and sexual assault was, and continues to be, enormously distressing at many levels, from the individuals involved, their families and friends, the wider community and in some instances the state and church. Following large-scale investigations, families both know and don't know what happened to their children/siblings/partners whilst in 'care'. We need to consider the impact on others when someone chooses to publish or publicly disclose their traumatic experiences which had previously been secret.

Some of the sibling groups I interviewed have never spoken with each other about their shared experience and continued to maintain their separate individual stories. In one family of three brothers – Paul, Robert and Steven – all placed at the same approved school in northwest England, they never talked with each other about what they had experienced. Paul shared his story with his sisters. Rob with his partner. Steven did not speak of it at all. This underlines that experiences within families and other shared contexts are uniquely different and individual. Paul, the eldest, felt guilty about not protecting his younger brothers, Rob and Steven. Neither Rob nor Steven felt he was responsible in any way for what happened to them. I became the holder of this knowledge which they were unable to share with each other – the 'transferential passageway' (Varela, 2001).

Differences between siblings or groups of people who have shared the same traumatic experience can produce a mixture of both positive and negative feelings. It can be very shocking to find such disparity in shared experiences. What one person may find traumatising another may not.

Families can demonstrate resilience in maintaining their narratives in 'the face of an unacceptably destabilising new story' (Sluzki, 2008, p. 126). Sometimes stability is more important than change and keeping these two influences – change and stability – in balance over the life cycle requires constant adjusting. Some of the factors associated with

resilient functioning in families relate to dominant beliefs, family structure and organisation, communication within families, and shared
pleasurable activities (Walsh, 2002). This can be elaborated by specifically asking about stories where the family has successfully dealt with
adversity.

Transmission of pattern over time and through generations is not
only a biological function but also a psychological one. Traumatic
narratives can be passed down through generations producing traumatic reactions in children where the only traumatic event is that the
parents were traumatised (Yehuda *et al.*, 1998a, b). Naomi Shragai, interviewed by the *Guardian* newspaper, describes her feelings growing up as
a child of parents who had survived the Holocaust. She talked of her
awareness of the trauma that was never spoken about but felt – a process
she called 'inexplicable osmosis'. The experience left her mother hypersensitive to any family separations (Shragai, 2007).

Developing a coherent narrative of traumatic experiences may take
several generations to achieve. A coherent narrative can be destabilised
or reorganised around life-cycle events. Claudia Poblete discovered as a
young adult that she was one of the children taken from their parents
who 'disappeared' in Argentina during great political upheaval between
1976 and 1983 and was given to a childless couple. Her grandmother,
part of the Abuelas de Plaza Mayo movement – grandmothers who
searched for their 'disappeared' grandchildren – found her. She
described her life-cycle transitions as helping her to think differently
about her own parents and her adopters. As she moved into her own
marriage with hopes of creating a family, she described a process of
constant re-evaluation of her lived experiences and relationships,
shaped as they were by a wider political discourse.

Claudia details her own journey to constructing a new identity. This
included considering and re-evaluating her previous identity and the
identities of those around her. Thus her 'parents' became her 'appropri-
ators'. This change in identities is captured in the example of Hazel, a
kinship carer, shown in Clinical vignette 2.1.

Hazel, who cares for her daughter's children, became very distressed
when her daughter had another child within another domestically
violent relationship. This challenged Hazel's idea of her daughter as a
helpless victim. When we discussed this, Hazel related the story of her
daughter's traumatic birth and how it made her feel that she needed to
protect her daughter.

Hazel could see that she had kept alive this idea of her daughter as a
special baby who needed to be protected literally and metaphorically.
She had taken on her daughter's children. She minimised her daughter's

CLINICAL VIGNETTE 2.1		
Speaker	**Spoken communication**	**Clinical reflections**
Hazel	I needed to move on from it.	Hazel is referring to the story of her daughter's birth. She is signalling that she is ready to consider other explanations for her daughter's behaviour.
Clinician	Why do you feel you have to move on?	This is an attempt to seek amplification or elaboration about the hypothesis that Hazel wants/needs to move on.
Hazel	Every time I tell the story of her birth, the pain is terrible.	This suggests that Hazel is still traumatised by the birth of her daughter – the story had become a reliving and had stopped not only Hazel from moving on but also her daughter growing up.
Clinician	How do you think this story of her birth shaped your relationship with your daughter?	This is a punctuation of the narrative and draws attention to Hazel's inability to move on.
Hazel	I hadn't thought about that ... I worried about her. I transferred that worry on to her. I worried constantly about her – she didn't eat enough; didn't do this or that ... I watched her sometimes ... I pushed her too much ... her lifestyle now means I still worry about her ... I have never been able to not worry about her ...	The question seems to push Hazel into 'new territory' in considering her relationship with her daughter.
Clinician	What effect do you think all this worry had on your daughter?	Hazel is being asked to consider her daughter's perspective.
		Continued

	CLINICAL VIGNETTE 2.1 *Continued*	
Speaker	**Spoken communication**	**Clinical reflections**
Hazel	Exactly the opposite effect I intended. She never really took responsibility for herself. I still do it now ... I am even looking after her children for her.	Hazel is reconsidering how her taking responsibility for her daughter has contributed to her daughter's inability to take responsibility for herself.

contribution to the unacceptable conditions her grandchildren were born into, preferring to blame her daughter's male partners.

Her grandchildren talked about how Hazel always put their mum first and made excuses for her. Helping Hazel think of the multiple roles she occupied (mother and grandmother being the focus of this discussion) and how she was more of a mother to her grandchildren then their mother was – enabled her to focus clearly on what aspect of her being was needed in each context. She was able to tell her grandchildren that their mother was still her daughter and she felt she had to care for her but that she also recognised she needed to stop defending her, especially to the children she (the daughter) had let down and that Hazel now cared for. This multiple perspective-taking is an aspect of resilience.

Hazel, in reflecting on the family stories she had grown up with, indicated that her relationship with her own mother remained important even after her mother had died. She describes the day she realised she needed to take responsibility for her own difficulties. This shows how relationships can change over time.

I used to talk to my mum at her grave. I'd ask her for help with my daughter. I went one time and thought to myself – here I am she's even dead and I'm bringing my troubles to her. I went up and said 'Mum I am sorry, just have a rest, sleep ... this is my problem'.

I wondered with Hazel if she ever imagined her daughter saying this to her.

The conversation in Clinical vignette 2.1 is helping Hazel to recognise that her story of her daughter has inadvertently become an objectification of her daughter as victim and has failed to recognise her daughter's perspective and personal agency.

Some trauma survivors (especially those abused in childhood) make choices not to have children as a way of breaking the perceived 'cycle of abuse'. The Ryan Report (2009) records that:

> Witnesses ... described parenting difficulties ranging from being over-protective to being harsh and commented on the intergenerational sequelae of their childhood abuse (Ryan Report, 2009, p. 14).

In reviewing work with adult survivors abused within the 'care system', as well as children currently in care, it appears that the intervention of the state disrupts and sometimes contradicts families' stories of themselves. The message of failure and shame is overwhelming. This is in part what drives Hazel to look after her grandchildren and demonstrate her family's resilience.

The opportunity for curiosity and reflection can be limited by adversarial court proceedings where partisan stories of what has happened are regularly relayed via third parties into a public arena. One mother describing her experience of child care court proceedings explained her experience metaphorically as:

> It's like they put you in a bull ring and run you round and around until you fall from exhaustion ...

Part of the self identity as a 'good enough parent' is denied. It can seem that nothing can change this perception of parental self. This example highlights how interventions aimed at putting something right for one part of the system can also be traumatising for another. The wider context can constrain conversations where mistakes could be acknowledged and discussed.

It is important that in promoting the idea of transgenerational transmission of trauma, we pay equal attention to the stories of resilience that are transmitted through generations.

Resilience and community action

Writing can be an act of resistance – a way of ensuring that a story is heard and not forgotten. Take for example Cecylia Slapakowa's interviews of Warsaw ghetto women as part of **Oyneg Shabes** (joyful Sabbath) collective which co-ordinated a project dedicated to recording life in the ghetto for future generations:

in the tragic destructive chaos of our present day life, we can nonetheless observe flashes of creative activity, the slow development and birth of forces that are building a base for the future. (Kassow, 2007, p. 13)

This clearly demonstrates 'adversity-activated development' (Papadopoulos, 2007). The stories and artefacts were collected and hidden to be found. Having this other in mind became part of the creative effort to maintain identity in an ever-shrinking, lethal environment.

The recognition at a wider social level of the trauma endured can be healing. However, it sometimes raises doubts or does not provide the vindication or acknowledgement commensurate with lived experience. Many adults abused in care made claims for compensation. This involved them retelling their stories of traumatic experiences. It has also sometimes meant they have reconnected with others who lived through the same experiences.

The compensation is over and done with. Us girls that left Ireland were not treated as fairly as we seemed to have managed rather better than those who stayed and been awarded less compensation ... (Angela)

Angela raises some important issues in her observation. Relocating after a trauma can help 'make a new life'. Reinventing 'self' in a new culture or a new language can facilitate recovery (Smith, 2005b). Such a dramatic change of context can allow for different and/or new aspects of self to emerge. The environmental stimuli to traumatic experience can also be reduced. Consider the example given earlier about Afia who as a refugee was learning to live in another country, in another language, surrounded by different scenes and smells. A traumatic experience is embedded within a context. The triggers to flashbacks or unwanted intrusive memories can be sights, sounds or smells that were present at the time of the trauma. Relocation to another country may reduce some of these. There can also be anonymity in a new context that would not be available otherwise. For example, Angela came from a small rural town where everyone knew where you came from and who your 'people' were.

Angela highlights a view that trauma and wellbeing are often seen as being along a single continuum. In her example this is reflected by lower compensation payments to those women who had left Ireland and seemed to be 'doing better'. This implies that the more resilient a person is, the less traumatised they are, as represented by smaller compensation awards.

Wider public inquiries and responses to shared traumatic experiences are now more commonplace. For example the Commission to Inquire into Child Abuse (CICA) was one of the measures put in place by the Irish government to consider the extent and effects of the abuse of children from 1936 onwards. Its 2009 report, the Ryan Report, documents the experiences of those raised in orphanages in Ireland.

It describes the children being treated like 'convicts and slaves'. Many levels of failure were identified in the extensive abuse in numerous institutions across Ireland and in other countries where the religious orders ran schools and orphanages.

Institutional abuse is by no means exclusively the province of religious orders. In Canada, for example, a Truth and Reconciliation Commission has been established for 'the child taken and the parent left behind' in response to the government-funded policy of removing aboriginal children from their families and communities and sending them to residential schools. A government policy of separating children from 'dysfunctional' parents underpinned the Irish orphanages – as many children were not orphaned at all. Wider public inquiries need to unearth the unspoken assumptions about when the state considers it has the right to intervene so dramatically in private family life.

Truth and Reconciliation Commissions are based on the idea of restorative justice which seeks to build relationships and re-establish shared responsibility for constructive responses to wrongdoing within communities. It involves both victims and perpetrators and includes witnesses to record and report on the work undertaken. Public inquiries sometimes focus more on blame rather than reparation.

The Abuelas de Plaza Mayo movement of grandmothers searching for their 'disappeared' children seeks restitution of kidnapped children to their legitimate families. The shared experience of traumatic events can forge strong relationships between people and mobilise them to protest about the secrecy and denial that surrounded these traumatic experiences.

It is important to be mindful of the wider political context into which stories of resilience and trauma are embedded. Arlene Healey (Healey, 2004; Reilly, 1999) describes how in family sessions in Northern Ireland there began to be 'talks about the talks'. The wider political context can affect what conversations may be allowed within families, and indeed communities, and allow narratives of resilience and resistance to emerge. Time can facilitate context change or promote a readiness to hear stories that may have been previously dismissed or denied. It was the lobbying of Vietnam War veterans that resulted in PTSD being included in the DSM.

Publicly held inquiries and commissions highlight the wider influences that led to individual experiences of pain and suffering. Acknowledging this wider context allows stories and voices to be heard and removes some of the fear and isolation produced by the traumatic experience. This collective storytelling becomes an active resistance to the overwhelming and silencing nature of trauma. It also addresses the wider community's shame for failing to prevent the systematic abuses that become a collective trauma.

In trauma work there will be political nuances that need attending to. 'Each person is born into a cluster of stories including the political, economic and cultural zeitgeist as well as personal, family and community obligations' (Hedges, 2005). The acronym GRRAACCES (gender, race, religion, age, ability, class, culture, education, sexuality) helps to highlight the multilayered, multiplexed, multistoreyed aspects of self that converge in the emergence of meaning making dialogues (Burnham *et al.*, 2008).

Political discourses make space for stories where blame is situational (wrong place at the wrong time) and are not so focused on 'characterological' blame ('I am a bad person, I deserved it.') (Andrews and Brewin, 1990). There were wider social patterns that influenced who was placed, for example, in the Irish orphanage. Sometimes it can be hard for the individual involved to see those wider political patterns.

There are not only psychological but also political aspects to the suppression of memory. Taking away a people's language and their stories of lived experience goes beyond colonisation. It becomes a form of cultural genocide. The political discourses and protest against these denials promotes and contributes to psychological resilience. This bigger pattern of suppression of memory is often enacted on the smaller microcosmic system of family. Shameful actions are the most likely candidates for systematic obliteration.

Conclusion

In providing a theoretical overview of resilience, clinicians can feel confident in discovering and uncovering resilient behaviours embedded in, but often hidden by, the traumatic experience. The meaning attributed to experience shapes stories of self, family and community.

Promoting resilience over generations requires dismantling ideas about the inevitability of repetitive re-enactments of traumatic experience. It means integrating the stories of victim and perpetrator. This 'both/and' positioning facilitates responsibility and support for recovery and resilience to emerge from traumatic experiences. It allows for the opportunity to consider wider social systems and the dominant discourse which include patterns of power and inequality within which the individual lived experience is embedded (Dallos and Urry, 1999).

An 'either/or' position allows for distance and difference to be created between participants in a potentially unhelpful way. This does not condone the perpetration of traumatic acts but seeks to recognise that the perpetration not only traumatises the recipient but also the perpetrator. We can move between 'either/or' and 'both/and' positions over the life course.

> I'm not sure we ever seek closure on our experiences. Somehow or other the past keeps coming up. ... I think as we go through life we do think differently. ... I can remember the excitement of getting married having my own children and feeling on top of the world. The only thought I had at that time was how could my mother have given me away. I do of course now understand why. There was a period of time when I gave little thought to my past as I had my own children and became engrossed in them. It was however around this time that my blood mother became important in my life ... I do think we look at things differently as we age. ... There is only one thing that I would have loved in life and that was to see my blood mother. I'm sure she too carried some regret regarding the baby she delivered and never again saw. I would have loved to tell her that what she had to do was OK and that I was not angry about what happened. (Angela).

This wonderfully compassionate reflection underscores that different life-cycle stages conjure up different and potentially more forgiving perspectives. We can in part influence whether trauma or resilience becomes the dominant theme of our life stories.

> I no longer have the anger that I had regarding my past however one never forgets but learns to live with it therefore in doing so we find peace as we are aware we can't change the past and will only destroy ourselves if we hold on to bitterness. ... I am very much at peace at the moment. (Angela).

This reflects acceptance in action.

PART 2

The Field of Practice

3

ENGAGEMENT AND CREATING A SAFE CONTEXT

Introduction

This chapter will focus on the issue of engagement and how to establish a sufficiently safe context for clients to allow narratives involving trauma to emerge, be contained and transformed. This includes attention to safety within the session, including managing situations that become unsafe, pacing within sessions, who to invite, containing intense emotions, and strengthening stories of resilience.

Engagement

Engagement refers to the initial stages of a therapeutic encounter where the client and clinician negotiate the work they are going to do together. This may mean explaining the theoretical approach as not all clients will have purposefully selected systemic approaches. This crucial part of therapy involves outlining confidentiality, the clinician's code of conduct and ensuring a clear understanding of what will be happening. Part of this process is ensuring a 'good-enough fit' between client and clinician.

Engagement is the prerequisite of establishing a safe context to allow new conversations to emerge and healing to take place. To begin working on traumatic experiences, it is essential to pay particular attention to this aspect of the therapeutic relationship, as the desire to avoid or not discuss traumatic material is very powerful. Hypervigilance and hyperarousal, both common in traumatised individuals, mean clients are on the alert for cues to 'fight or take flight'. It can make it difficult to seek help and/or remain in therapy. Maria captures this in her reflections about what worked for her.

> I was always looking for faults with the kind of therapy or with the therapist, so that I could make an excuse not to continue what we'd started as it was all too much for me to deal with at times. I was frightened about what might come up or need to be discussed. Part of me knew I needed to talk about it but another part really didn't want to.

This avoidance of engaging with traumatic material may not only be an issue for the client. Clinicians can be cautious in raising traumatic material in an effort to avoid causing additional distress to clients. However, waiting for clients to spontaneously raise traumatic material may mean it never comes up directly in the therapeutic process. This is part of the avoidance aspect of a PTSD.

When working in a family context, it may be difficult to know who knows what about the traumatic experience. Consideration needs to be given to the issue of privacy, boundaries and managing distress both within sessions and between sessions. This should be discussed at the outset and reviewed periodically throughout the clinical work as circumstances change. It may be helpful to meet parents first, to ensure they are able to manage conversations that involve their children and exposure to traumatic events.

Thomas and his partner came to therapy because of the difficulties associated with Thomas's childhood experiences of abuse. Linda, his partner, supported him. She knew about 'his past'. Initially they wanted to work together but as Thomas began disclosing more detail about his past, Linda felt less comfortable hearing it. In therapy, we discussed what it would mean to their relationship if Thomas carried on working without her present in the room. Linda was concerned that Thomas would think she was less supportive. Thomas was frightened that Linda would be disgusted and no longer want to be in a relationship with him. Together they were able to discuss how to move forward in the therapeutic process. Thomas had some sessions on his own, and Linda and he would regularly have a joint session. This allowed Linda to remain supportive and Thomas to feel able to disclose disturbing aspects of his lived experience without feeling he might jeopardise his relationship. It generated interesting discussions for the couple about 'needing to know everything about each other'. So while Linda knew about Thomas's past, how it impacted on the here-and-now of their relationship was more important to her than knowing the detail. This example illustrates the complex interplay of time and relationship.

The client's journey into therapy

Considering how the client came to therapy should inform the engagement process. In the interests of transparency, it is important to share referral information. This sometimes helps to flag up traumatic material at the outset that can be explored in more detail later. Referral letters often identify a significant past event that is thought to be possibly connected to current difficulties.

Many people enter therapy because of feelings or 'symptoms' that they may not connect with a traumatic experience. This may be especially true for referrals of children and adolescents where it is often adults who identify a problem they think the child or young person should work on.

Many adult survivors of the care system did not consider the impact of these traumatic experiences in shaping their lives. For them, that was just the way it was and had been for many years. Exposure to chronic trauma, and the inevitable accommodation to it, can mean individuals take certain behaviours as normal because it is hard for them to remember a time when they did not behave like this.

Making use of symptoms

Symptoms can be seen as useful resources when helping clients to change their lives. Seeing them as a 'resource' is an example of reframing – a systemic technique where a different point of view is suggested that allows someone to consider different approaches with this new 'frame' (Haley, 1973; Watzlawick *et al.*, 1974). A complete discussion of reframing is beyond the scope of this book, but it plays a significant role in many forms of psychotherapy, including systemic approaches. Historically it is associated with the four major schools of family therapy – the Mental Research Institute (MRI) model of brief **strategic therapy** (Fisch *et al.*, 1982; Watzlawick *et al.*, 1974); strategic family therapy (Haley, 1987; Madanes, 1982); structural family therapy (Minuchin and Fishman, 1981); and Milan systemic family therapy (Boscolo *et al.*, 1987; Selvini, 1988).

Currently systemic therapists work hard to avoid '**problem-saturated narratives**' or stories that focus too much or exclusively on difficulties and problems without paying sufficient attention to aspects of resilience and resistance. Conclusions drawn from problem-saturated stories can disempower clients as they tend to focus on or see symptomatic behaviours as weaknesses, disabilities, dysfunctions or inadequacies (Morgan, 2000).

However, making connections between current symptomatic behaviours and past traumatic events may be extremely important in understanding how the situation came to be as it is and how it can be changed. This was the strategic maxim that the current problem was a solution to a previous problem that has not evolved or adapted to changing circumstances.

Unacknowledged trauma has a way of reasserting its shaping influence on our lives through 'inexplicable' episodes of anxiety and distress, both physical and emotional. This is the moving between past and present time that trauma can activate. Because systemic psychotherapists may be working with family groups, each individual may have a different time perspective on events. What may be an issue in the past for one person, may be very much 'alive' and in the present for another.

Understanding the system's initial position

Peter Stratton (2003) discusses the importance of understanding the family's explanations regarding the 'presenting' problem or what has brought the family to seek therapeutic help. If the experience of entering family therapy is too different from their expectation, they may be unable to engage.

Clinical vignette 3.1 is an excerpt from the first minutes of a family therapy session. Julio (10) has been referred because of his feelings of distress and upset (the presenting problem) following his parents separation (the trigger). The referral letter also indicated that domestic violence was the trigger for the separation (a potentially traumatic experience). The clinician needs to be mindful of who is present in the session and who is not, and the roles they occupy. In this case, three generations are present as Julio has come with his mother and his maternal grandmother. The clinician may have ideas about how the domestic violence has impacted on this family. There are gender issues as the father is not present and no other male relative attended. Life-cycle issues are also present, in particular for the boy, now 10, who is about to begin his journey to manhood but also for the grandmother who finds herself looking after her grown daughter again. The clinician might be curious about how the journey to manhood is negotiated between mother and son following the likely traumatic disruption of the marital relationship and possibly what this situation means for the previous generation – grandmother and mother who are also mother and daughter. In the first instance, it is clear that working as a family was not what they were expecting.

CLINICAL VIGNETTE 3.1		
Speaker	**Spoken conversation**	**Clinical reflections**
Clinician	What ideas did you have about coming here today?	When children are referred, parents are often surprised that they are asked to be involved in the treatment. Asking about expectations helps to correct any misinterpretations and consider how you might work together.
Mother	I just thought ... it would be more for Julio to be honest. I didn't think we would be sat in on it.	Sometimes it is not clear whether parents know what is contained in referral letters. Asking what she thought should be talked about with Julio might help. However this can lead to pressure being put on the child to talk about the *problems* they are causing or having.
Clinician	So what ideas do you have about why we think it is important to work with you as a family?	Returning to ask mother underlines and acknowledges her authority within the family. Following domestic violence, maternal authority is often undermined and needs to be reinstated.
Mother	So we can all see how each other is feeling and help each other?	This provides an emerging relational narrative and raises the theme of 'helping each other' – a resilience factor.
Clinician	(nods and turns to grandma) How about yourself?	The nonverbal behaviour acknowledges the contribution. Turning to the other adult in the room further underlines the responsibility of adults to make this context meaningful to the child.
		Continued

Speaker	Spoken conversation	Clinical reflections
CLINICAL VIGNETTE 3.1 *Continued*		
Grandma	I didn't expect to be sitting in with them. I am glad that I am because there are things that my daughter may not pick up on that I notice. Maybe I could learn to understand Julio a little more as well because he and his mum live with me. If I can help that bit more with Julio it releases a little bit of pressure off my daughter ... so I think we will all learn.	This provides new information. It was not clear that the family were living with maternal grandmother. She is clearly a resource and can help to provide another perspective to what has clearly been a difficult time for her daughter and grandson. It also demonstrates family resilience. It sets a positive frame of learning from each other and indicates a new family organisational structure is currently in place.

Linking the reason for referral – Julio's distress – with working together as a family is vital to keep the family engaged. Often parents find it easier to come for help for their children but are not ready to discuss the shared traumatic experience, in this case domestic violence, with them.

Moving between layers of context can help establish different points of view for the same experience. This broadens the traumatic perspective which tends to be narrow, fragmentary and focused on survival. It signals a new phase in the process of coming to terms with what has been survived. It also reinforces the resiliencies within the system.

Establishing a safe context

In considering using narrative approaches specifically, it is essential to consider safety issues. Allan Carr (2000a, p. 31) raises this issue specifically in cases where there may be 'crises involving immediate threats to clients' safety or the safety of family members'. Just telling 'the story', without attending to safety, raises ethical issues. For example, in working with domestic violence or self harm, specifically discussing safety issues is an important and necessary first step.

By exploring trauma narratives without first discussing, improving and developing stories of resistance, resilience and coping, we can tip clients into unsafe dangerous post-therapy contexts. In working with relational trauma, it is important to be explicit about therapeutic boundaries and the professional code of conduct that guides clinicians' practice. What can be kept within the confidentiality of the therapeutic relationship and what cannot needs to be made explicit. It may also need to be revisited over time.

It is helpful to overtly establish safety contracts in work involving, for example: self-harming behaviours; domestic violence; drug and alcohol abuse, and rehearsing how these 'safety nets' can be activated if therapeutic conversations stir up overwhelming feelings. Additionally, it may be useful to do a 'safety check' at the end of each session – ensuring that everyone feels relaxed and able to readjust to the change in context.

Safety issues should be raised at the outset of therapeutic trauma work. It can take the form of direct questions such as: 'Is there anything I need to know about what you do to manage overwhelming feelings?' This should be followed up with specific reference to the here and now of the session, for example: 'How might you let me know that what we are talking about is giving rise to overwhelming feelings?'

Eliana Gil (1996) wrote of how important it is for the clinician to be rested, relaxed and physically and psychologically ready to do the work. Many of the treatment models that work specifically with trauma focus on 'resource installation' or coping strategies (**eye movement desensitisation and reprocessing (EMDR)** or **dialectical behaviour therapy (DBT)**, for example). Systemic psychotherapists need to ensure a safe enough environment has been created for clients to begin to work on traumatic material. It is also important to prevent clients from being re-traumatised by the treatment experience or enacting/re-enacting harmful behaviours triggered by therapeutic sessions.

Barry Mason (1993, 2005) has developed the ideas of 'safe uncertainty' and 'authoritative doubt' to reflect the establishment of a context where the client can safely explore issues which the clinician may have some expertise about.

Some of the more postmodern approaches (Andersen, 1987, 1997; Anderson and Goolishian, 1992) seem to marginalise or minimise the role of expertise and professional experience in the therapeutic encounter. In these models the clinician is the conversational partner, not the 'expert' (Boston, 2000). Clinical experience and expertise can become an unconscious proficiency – where it becomes difficult for the clinician to 'not know what they know'. Using reflective process (Burnham, 1992) helps clinicians consider prejudices that influence practice. Clinicians and clients can share areas of expertise with the client as an expert on their experience and the clinician as an 'expert' across a topic such as trauma. Together they can draw upon each other's knowledge and expertise to create a new understanding of the individual experience as well as contributing to collective experience.

Enabling trauma narratives to be told

In narrative approaches, fostering an interest in the many stories that are present, rather than just the story told, allows for multiple frames of a single experience to interplay with a single frame of multiple experiences. Moving between these different points of view helps develop coherence and flexibility, something trauma, with its narrow point of view, constricts.

Families arrive with expectations about the therapeutic process often informed by previous experiences of counselling/therapy. Clinicians need to consider these expectations respectfully and be mindful of how they influence the therapeutic conversations that unfold (Epston and White, 1992).

It is important to be prepared to take **relational risks** in clinical work (Mason, 2005). This means moving into positions of uncertainty or areas of discomfort with clients. This is intended to produce a therapeutic edge where difference (something new) can be introduced. Difference is seen as an essential component of the change process. There are potential risks to clients and clinicians when doing this. Retelling a traumatic experience in and of itself is not necessarily healing. Sometimes it can be harmful, as the client can become more sensitised to the narrative and overwhelmed by the experience again. Clinicians can also be overwhelmed by traumatic stories. Clients need to have a 'felt experience' of being listened to or heard. If repetition of the story produces no new information or affective response this can be experienced as unhelpful and possibly re-traumatising.

Maria, in considering her experiences of therapy for traumatic life events, offers the following observations.

A safe place for me entailed a series of meetings with a therapist with specialist training in the particular field of concern for me. I was never interested in meeting with a counsellor *just as a sympathetic ear*, as I felt only someone who'd had similar experiences to me, or someone who'd had specialist training, would know how to guide me through all the negativity. It was also very important to me that the clinician had a good few years experience under their belt, as I once ended up many years ago at X hospital by self refer- ral and met a lovely Dr. He passed me over to one of his team members, a kindly Spanish girl of about 25, the same age as I was then, who struggled with speaking English, drew lots of flow charts on a flip board, and proceeded to conclude that I was a man-hater after six sessions. She really was of no help to me at all, and I was so disillusioned. It put me off attempting to get help for a few years. So if I were to summarise – professional, expertise and experience were the linch pins in making me feel safe and comfortable.

In reading Maria's comment on safe therapeutic spaces, it is important to consider those aspects of self that are visible or audible when meet- ing and beginning clinical work. Discussions about these aspects of self, often referred to by the acronym GRRAACCCES (Burnham, 1992, p. 24; Burnham *et al.*, 2008) need to be attended to in the engagement process.

Sometimes, important issues that might get in the way of therapeu- tic conversations are not mentioned. Maria mentions, for example, her counsellor's age and how this was similar to her own age at the time. This similarity made Maria feel less comfortable. Perhaps if it had been discussed, it could have been used creatively within the ther- apeutic process. Guilfoyle (2003) talks about how aspects of self can be 'concealed in its visibility', making it difficult to raise or discuss but still remaining very influential in shaping the conversations that can be had. This can be especially true if an 'expert' position is taken. Guilfoyle (2003) would typify an expert discourse as monologic rather than dialogic – one way commentary on someone else's experience. For some clients, this can create an initial sense of safety but may not be helpful in generating lasting change or transformation over time.

Safety within the therapeutic process is not static and needs to be reviewed, monitored and reflected on throughout the experience. Working regularly with a team or supervisor can ensure everyone's safety is kept in mind. As traumatic material arises, clients are likely to feel increasingly unsafe and rely on the clinician to help maintain a context that allows the work to proceed with just enough difference/discomfort to promote and allow something transformative to emerge.

Safe space in sessions

Entering into a therapeutic encounter where a traumatic narrative is anticipated, the clinician may benefit from considering the actual space where the meeting is being held; the position of the chairs; whether tissues are available. The size of the room may seem too small or too big. A lack of privacy may make it difficult to talk about fearful or shameful issues. Sometimes the traditional 'opposing chairs setup' can feel too confrontational or intense for the client.

Finding the right distance to conduct therapeutic work and introducing a feedback system that allows monitoring safety over time should be part of the initial contract. This may include moving seating positions within sessions. Consider the traditional face to face positioning of dyadic work, compared to a more side-by-side positioning in family work, because of the multiple participants. Early structural therapists often literally moved family members to new positions within a session by changing seating positions or using family sculpts to help illustrate or illuminate the 'positions' taken around an issue. These active methods of engaging with material need to be considered in light of traumatic narratives, where clients can be frozen or fixed in their experience and might perceive such activity as potentially threatening.

Outside of sessions, reflecting on structural elements such as preferred postures within sessions can provide information that can be used to open up the space for traumatic stories to be told and heard. Clinicians can convey inadvertently a bodily unwillingness to hear the story. A client with a traumatic narrative is likely to be hypervigilant to any signs of impending danger. They can misread signs and are more likely to perceive a situation as unsafe given their past experiences.

Fredman (2004, 2007) refers to **'emotional presupposing'** or imagining the likely emotional flow of the therapeutic conversation before the session begins. The idea of emotional presupposing is further developed (Fredman, 2007) into **'emotional postures'**, where consideration is given to the nonverbal messages that the clinician's body conveys to the client.

Consider, for example, children who have been sexually abused whilst being video recorded having their therapy sessions in a room set up with video equipment. Even if it's turned off, the video equipment can trigger traumatic re-enactments or produce a frozen watchfulness.

Safe pace in sessions

In clinical work, time and timing is crucial. Time will be experienced in different ways by different individuals, groups and even by the same person at different moments (Boscolo and Bertrando, 1992). The original Milan group (Selvini Palazzoli *et al.*, 1980) noted the focus on past events as causing current difficulties. As their work developed, the focus on future possibilities became a standard part of their interventions. This is referred to as '**hypothetical future questions**' (Boscolo *et al.*, 1987).

One of the symptoms of PTSD is a sense of a foreshortened future. Many clients who have experienced traumatic events 'live as if they have no future ... remain[ing] impoverished with respect to future alternatives and choices' (Tomm, 1987, p. 173). How we move through these time zones requires skill and judgement. It may first be necessary to abandon concepts of linear time and allow time to be flexible and fluid. Flexibility and fluidity are both seen as attributes of resilience. Moving between time past, present and future can allow issues to be addressed indirectly more safely and from the distance perspective can give. This promotes the meta-cognitions or thoughts about thoughts (stories about stories) that are often absent when traumatic narratives take over.

As thought precedes the action and verbalisation is articulating thought, conversations can become not only dangerous but also transforming. The movement between times allows the connections between events to be re-examined and re-evaluated. Future oriented stories can be activating and help transformations to manifest.

Shifting between time frames can help move the focus of a session from high-expressed emotions to less heated ones. Talking about traumatic events can activate symptoms including flashbacks, depression and anxiety. In family therapy, the greater number of participants (with shared stories and habitual patterns of interacting) means a session can quickly become dominated by unhelpful and potentially destructive patterns of interaction.

Working with sub-systems

Therapeutically, it may be helpful to work with sub-systems of the family and consider what issues will be discussed in the family sessions. For example, when and how to involve parents when children have been traumatized. When whole families have experienced a shared trauma such as war, natural disaster or domestic violence, different aspects of the shared experience will stand out as peak episodes for each family member. It may be too difficult to work on the material together as a family group. When working with families who have shared a traumatic event together, despite their shared experience they will each have individual perspectives on what happened.

Emmanuela was referred to a local CAMH service for night terrors. She and her family were refugees from Kosovo. This part of her story highlights how a single event can be viewed very differently by different family members.

Emmanuela was separated from her parents when they were fleeing from fighting in their village in Kosovo. Her parents felt guilty about this. Added to this, when they found Emmanuela later, they had shouted at her for getting separated from them. After some individual sessions, a family session was organised. It had been clear in her individual work that Emmauela had felt an increased sense of self-efficacy because she had taken care of herself, escaped and found her parents later. This needed to be shared in a family session. It highlighted Emmanuela's resilience. When her parents heard her account of the separation for the first time, it dramatically changed how they felt. She told them she felt she could and did manage on her own and that she didn't blame them for becoming separated. The huge sense of guilt the parents felt for losing Emmanuela in the mayhem had stopped them from asking about it. This exchange also allowed them to share other experiences and correct misperceptions they had carried since leaving Kosovo years earlier. It allowed her parents to apologise for getting separated and for shouting at her later when they found her. The family discussion facilitated the transformation of experience and strengthened the family's story of resilience.

This example shows the importance of establishing boundaries and considering the question of audience in therapy sessions. Many parents can misunderstand the context of family therapy as an invitation to talk 'in front of the children' about family life rather than talking with the children. If this involves traumatic material, the unboundaried discussion can increase stress and distress. If the parent is still traumatised themselves, as is often the case in domestic violence for example, it can be difficult for them to perceive the shared experience from any perspective other than their own and to forget that witnesses can be traumatised as well. This is sometimes referred to as '**vicarious trauma**', where someone experiences overwhelming distress from witnessing the traumatisation of someone else. This can also lead to '**survivor guilt**', where someone feels they should not have been spared from the traumatic experience. Within families, these experiences of 'survivor guilt' and 'vicarious traumatisation' are likely to be present.

Olivia was in family therapy to help her children come to terms with the recent split from their father who had been violent to her. In the sessions she sometimes began talking to the clinician as if the children were not present. Given the content of the material, this was unhelpful but demonstrated the strongly held belief that the 'children didn't know' what had gone on. In a way, Olivia was re-enacting what had already happened by talking about the violence in front of the children as if the children could not hear. Olivia was provided with a way of discriminating 'what was for big ears and what was for little ears'. She was prompted and reminded that 'little ears' were present when she began to move into her own traumatic material. This reinforced generational positions and helped Olivia maintain her role as parent. It also opened up the discussion about what the children had witnessed, including the consideration that witnessing is not solely a visual experience. The children described 'hearing' the violence and 'feeling guilty for not coming out of their room to help mummy'. Olivia, when she heard this, was able to reassure the children that it was not their responsibility to stop daddy from hurting her. She also sought some 'big ears' for herself.

This idea of generational boundaries seems less attended to in postmodern social constructionist models. It is often seen as an idea associated with strategic and structural approaches, which emphasised clear generational boundaries (Corey, 2009, p. 419; Draper and Dallos, 2010). Helping parents to think about how to talk with their children about traumatic events is extremely important. It may be helpful to consider how the child might have experienced the traumatic event. Many parents, in wanting to spare their children from traumatic material, convince themselves that the children were unaware of the danger. Parents need to think from a child's perspective and consider what aspects of a traumatic story the child needs to know at this point.

Jasmin (eight years old) was referred following her mother's arrest. Jasmin was placed with relatives pending the court case. Everyone felt Jasmin needed to be told what was happening. I met with Jasmin's grandparents and her mother separately due to court constraints. In conversation with the adults, I suggested that it was usually better for children to receive explanations from those people who are significant in their lives rather than strangers, even professional strangers like myself. I asked them who they thought was the best person to tell Jasmin what was happening. Her mother wanted to tell her and Jasmin's grandparents also felt her mother was the right person to tell

Jasmin what was happening. This was an indication of a good relationship between mother and daughter, supported by other significant family members. The wider professional system was focused exclusively on Jasmine's mother as an offender.

In family sessions with the mother and her parents, we discussed a range of different explanations. I offered advice, reminding them to keep it child-focused, age-appropriate and consider how Jasmin might hear the story. It was really impressive how the family worked together, making a space for Jasmin to know what she needed to know in a way that was respectful of Jasmin and her mother's relationship, despite the current crisis.

What a parent thinks will be traumatising for the child may be entirely different from what the child thinks.

Jasmin listened to her mother's explanation of why she was living with her grandparents. When given the opportunity to ask questions, Jasmine focused on the here and now – How long will I live with nanny and granddad? When is the court case? When can I live back at home with you?

This demonstrates the multiple layers of resilience within which the story unfolded. Jasmin was a happy, easy-going, active young girl with many friends and extracurricular activities, living at home with her mum in a secure parent–child relationship with regular close daily contact with an extended family of aunts, uncles, cousins and maternal grandparents. When the arrest occurred, Jasmin's extended family was able to offer a safe place for her while the legal process carried on.

Feeling unsafe or threatened

When working with traumatic material it is easy for feelings to become overwhelming. Often these overwhelming feelings can manifest in the session triggered by the discussion. An external constraint placed by a wider system can construct a time frame that is not best for the client. Managing the tensions between two systems, the client's internal narrative and the narrative required by a wider system, makes working systemically so intricate. Systems' time is not uniformly linear and it is easy to become preoccupied with for example 'court time' at the expense of 'client time'. This can lead to an inattention to what is going on in the 'here and now' that can lead to unsafe situations.

Kathy was asked to see me by her solicitor to prepare a report for compensation following a serious sexual assault. I did a home visit. This immediately raises the issue of how we keep ourselves safe when working in the community. Although we may have policies and procedures regarding this, the importance of tracking what is happening in the conversation is often overlooked.

As Kathy began talking about what happened to her, she became upset. She stood up and began pacing the room. With the benefit of hindsight I can see that this was a signal to me that the session was perhaps proceeding too quickly. Kathy was becoming agitated as she recounted what had happened. This was another sign to me that she was not recounting what had happened to her, she was beginning to relive it, with me as a witness. I remember her standing in the kitchen looking out the window filled with emotion. I am not sure she was speaking to me but she picked up a carving knife and turned to me. 'He shouldn't have treated me that way. I should have stabbed him.' She was now shouting about her perpetrator waving a knife around. I was sitting on the settee filled with terror and dread. Although fear and dread were the dominant emotions for me, I can remember my inner dialogue – 'She is not angry with you. She is angry with him for what he did to her'.

This demonstrates the inner voice of the clinician at work (Rober, 2005) or reflection in action (Schön, 1995) with different discourses emerging suggesting different courses of action.

I said her name. This underlines the importance of establishing contact in the here and now. It also emphasised her as a person with an identity, which sexual assault often annihilates. This established eye gaze. Sometimes this can be too intense in sessions, so judgement is needed to decide when this is helpful. It helps to consider tone of voice and the breath – can you maintain a 'posture of tranquillity' at such times? (Friedman, 1995, p. 97; Spellman and Smith, 2010, p. 89). In situations that are emotionally charged, escalation and mobilisation by the client are likely.

'Kathy, I know you are angry with him for what he did (acknowledging her feelings and who they were directed towards). He shouldn't have done that to you. You didn't deserve what happened to you. It was not your fault.' Kathy started to calm down. She put the knife down and sat beside me. This parallel seating disengaged eye contact and produced a postural congruence between us. Previously she had been standing up and I had been sitting. She began to talk about how she had felt it was her fault; how she thought she had brought it upon herself; and that she was undeserving of any compensation or recognition as a victim of crime.

Had I fled in fear or ended the session, this part of our conversation may not have happened. It provided an opportunity for us to consider these ideas and how they were holding up her recovery.

There can be times when a clinician can feel threatened both physically and psychologically.

Mr Baxter wanted contact with his six-year-old son. He was involved in court proceedings. There were numerous unproven allegations about his behaviour and numerous reports by experts recommending no further contact. Mr Baxter attended his appointment with his older son (19). When they came into the interview room, they remained standing with coats on. They were both considerably taller and physically larger than I was. They refused to sit down, preferring to pace about the room. This emphasised the physical differences in size between us. Mr Baxter had his hand in his jacket pocket and was indicating to me he had something concealed there. He was speaking heatedly about the other experts he had seen and how he was 'going to show them'. He would encourage his eldest son to tell me what a good father he was. I experienced Mr Baxter, and to a lesser extent his son, as intimidating. I felt unable to begin a conversation with the two of them pacing the room; coats on and hinting at what was inside the jacket pocket. When I asked them to take their coats off and sit down, they refused. It was clear they didn't want to be there and attended the appointment because they felt they had to.

In reflecting back on this example, working in a team or with a co-worker may have been useful. It is possible that the intention of attending was expressly to threaten and intimidate. This seems strange as the behaviour they exhibited was the least likely to result in contact being considered in the best interests of the child. There was no engagement and no safe context could be negotiated to begin to discuss how he might reconnect with his son.

Another example relates to an interview with a care survivor, Andrew. As he began to talk of the abuse he had suffered in care he became increasingly upset and angry at what had happened to him. His childhood abuse was perpetrated by adult men. This specific aspect of the sexual abuse, same-sex perpetrators, disturbed him. He was concerned that I might see him as homosexual as a consequence of his experiences. Once he raised the issue of homosexuality, he began a long monologue of extreme homophobic vitriol and hate speech that I was unsuccessful in stopping or punctuating. The interview felt dangerous. I moved away from the discussion about his traumatic experiences and ended the session discussing more neutral and less distressing topics.

Trying to address such deeply held prejudices in therapy is challenging. I had failed to establish a context in which we were able to co-create local meanings (Lyotard, 1984).

This may include the nonverbal signals clients share with us. Clients can also indicate, through nonverbal behaviours, that sessions are too slow. Trauma work tends to oscillate between these two polarities. Clients can want to 'blurt' out the whole story on the one hand, like Andrew, or avoid discussing it at all, like Mr Baxter, who wanted contact with his 6-year-old son but wasn't prepared to talk about.

From monologue to dialogue

Finding a way to hear traumatic material that allows it to be discussed and dialogic rather than monologic, helps clients reposition themselves in relation to their lived experience. The material can be talked about conversationally, which allows reflection on experience which may have previously not been possible. For Andrew and Mr Baxter, this kind of reflective conversation was not possible and possibly not wanted as they both attended interviews as part of a wider process that compelled them to attend. The fit between clinician and client may not have been good enough. Both cases cross the gender divide – male client/female clinician.

Sometimes 'the practice of silence' (Sheehan, 2007) is the best intervention. The silence between words can add to comprehension. Silence punctuates. It also helps to slow the session down. Often systemic approaches do not focus enough on the physical aspects of work – how the body and physiological systems interact with the narratives presented within the therapeutic arena (Griffith and Griffith, 1994).

Traumatic narratives will move quickly in and out of the here and now. There will be a constant sifting through multiple layers of material and emotions that emerge within the therapeutic relationship. Remembering to use the multiple identities that are simultaneously present and the useful movement between time – past, present and future – can help to regulate the emotional tone of a session.

Decision-making is part of the dialogical self (Bertrando, 2007). There will be a constant interplay and adjustment between clinician and client as together they work toward new ways of being. The pull to embody the dilemmas presented in trauma work – to enact the fight or flight response – is ever present. Keeping this tendency within the limits of safety allows the emergence of resilient narratives.

Affect regulation in sessions

Clients with traumatic narratives are hypervigilant and hyperaroused, watching for signs of any impending danger. They are on the lookout for perceived threats, provocations and expressions of scorn which map on to the emotions of fear, anger and shame respectively. Naming or acknowledging these feelings can help the movement to safer positions and allow conversations to emerge from the momentary affect laden silence.

Affect regulation has become a key theme in trauma work. In family therapy this can be complex as there will be a range of emotions from a number of different participants, including children. Clinicians and teams will also impact on the emotional tone of a session (Spellman and Smith, 2010).

It is important to respect the client's pace. This can be easier to do in sessions with individuals. Pacing can be slowed down by reflecting on what has been understood so far, inviting correction and further reflections before moving on. Clinical vignette 3.2 demonstrates an attempt to establish a safe context and consider pacing in a family session. Present in the session is a mother, her 13-year-old daughter and her nine-year-old son. They have been referred from a women's refuge.

While this excerpt from an initial session helps establish a context of safety, it will be necessary to revisit and renegotiate what can and cannot be discussed with her son who 'doesn't know'. This constitutes the therapeutic edge that needs to emerge to allow different stories to be told. The mother, by not sharing all that has happened, could be trying to preserve her son's relationship with his father. However, ongoing contact with his father could jeopardise his mother's safety. These tensions need to be explored. Entering into this conversational realm is an example of relational risk taking.

CLINICAL VIGNETTE 3.2		
Speaker	**Spoken conversation**	**Clinical reflections**
Clinician	Is this a very difficult area to think about?	Mum has begun to get tearful in the session.
Mother	Nodding	This is moving out of the realm of worded conversation.
Clinician	Is it comfortable going there today?	This is checking out whether mother feels able to carry on with the conversation.
Mother	No, No.	She is becoming more distressed.

Speaker	Spoken conversation	Clinical reflections
Clinician	Okay that's important for me to understand ... if we are touching on areas that you think are too painful to discuss right now we can think about how and when you might talk about this with your children. How are you going to let me know? I noticed a look between you and your daughter ...	Acknowledging her distress is important especially as she is here with her children. The introduction of 'right now' allows for the possibility of another time. Commenting on the nonverbal messages of the session suggesting perhaps mother and daughter have a connection not shared by the son moves into a different relational frame.
Mother	It's just he doesn't know.	This strengthens the hunch that the boy is in some way excluded from 'knowing'. Saying this in front of her son, will heighten his anxiety as he is likely to know quite a lot even if she thinks he doesn't. This is the realm of family secrets.
Clinician	Maybe there are conversations for grownups to hear that little boys don't need to hear right now ... I'll be guided by you. To the sister: What do you think your mum is worried about?	Underlining the generational positions within the room helps to reinforce maternal authority. Asking for reflections from a different perspective through the sister on the family secret is an invitation to open up and unpack a 'family secret'.
Sister	He keeps asking when he is going to see dad. He doesn't understand what's going on.	This demonstrates the different perspectives within a family and how these can cause tensions between members. It may also heighten a gender divide with mothers and daughters as females closely connected and removed from in this case sons and brothers as males because of gendered stories about husbands.

Safety issues in sessions

On reflection, important themes and issues arise. Gender issues arise in many of the examples which are drawn from the field of relational trauma. This is perhaps not surprising. Safety issues in work need to be constantly reviewed in light of personal and professional life-cycle issues. Working in a team can be helpful in containing strong feelings and strengthening the safety and containment aspects of trauma work. Teams can hold and represent a diversity of views and life-cycle positions. A team may be able to provide a bridge or link to lived experience that keeps the work safely in the here and now.

In certain chronically stressed contexts (like war or protracted court proceedings) individuals experience a reduction in the repertoires of self to one or a few powerful positions as a reaction to complexities or uncertainties (Frosh, 1997; Hermans and Dimaggio, 2007). Traumatic experiences will also narrow the repertoire of self as the individual becomes focused on survival even after the traumatic context has changed. So, for example, a woman who has been abused by her husband can forget she is also a mother.

Family sessions can also pose risks to family members. Sometimes it may be necessary to establish a contract of safety for couples or families between sessions (Goldner *et al.*, 1990; Groen and Van Lawick, 2009).

When working with traumatic material, enactments can be triggered in the session. If a client's habitual way of managing their feelings is through self harm or violence to others, it is important to consider this in therapeutic work. These situations may require active intervention.

For example, I was working with a mother, Sue, and her two children Toby (three years) and Ruth (one year). Sue was working toward having Toby and Ruth live with her after a period in care following an injury to Toby. Sue had been in care herself from a young age. She was still very young – only 21. She was living on her own with no extended family or partner to support her. I was observing Sue's contact. Sue was on the floor playing with her children.

The session began with Sue getting out toys for the children. Toby grabbed one of the toys. Sue told him to put it down. He refused. She took the toy away and he hit her. Sue told him off. Ruth was toddling about and Sue asked for a cuddle. Ruth didn't want to be held so she resisted and in doing so threw her head back and hit Sue on the nose. In that moment Sue snapped, lifting her hand to hit Ruth. I jumped up, saying 'Let me help you'. I moved closer to Sue and knelt on the floor – a postural congruence. Ruth toddled off to play. Toby was absorbed with the toys. I continued: 'It's really hard managing little children and it hurts when they hit you. You're working so hard and all you seem to get is hit'. Sue began crying. 'All my life I have been hit. I can't bear it that even my children hit me'.

Remaining in the passive observer position could have resulted in a child being hit in the session. Connecting with Sue's experience as a parent and supporting her allowed her to talk about her own miserable childhood and her experience of failure as a parent. She could see how her past was getting in the way of her being the parent she wanted to be.

Ophelia, a teenage girl who had experienced violence and sexual abuse, began to talk about what had happened to her. She started to arrive for her sessions drunk. We discussed this. Her relationship with drink was becoming significantly more intrusive and impeding on her therapeutic work. I don't think I considered this enough, believing that if we could discuss the traumatic material, her need to self medicate (as I understood her relationship with drink) would lessen. I also considerably underestimated how serious her addiction was. I had asked Ophelia's mother to bring her to and from the sessions to support her and ensure she arrived without having a drink.

During one session, as we began talking, Ophelia became increasingly anxious. 'I can't do this', she said. 'I need a drink'. Before I had understood what she had said, Ophelia had pulled out a small bottle of spirits. I apologised for not managing the situation well enough for her. I could see I was going too quickly and I had not recognised that her coping strategies were so addictive. I told her she couldn't drink here and asked her to put it away. I invited her mother into the session. We discussed how drink was taking over Ophelia's life and that it wasn't possible for more sessions to continue until her relationship with drink was under control, as talking about what happened to her triggered more drinking.

Working with Ophelia demonstrates the movement between allowing her developmentally appropriate autonomy as a teenager and reinstating effective parental presence (Omer, 2000, p. 82). Ophelia's mother felt responsible for Ophelia's traumatic experience and found it hard to enforce appropriate boundaries and restrictions on her behaviours. She felt sorry for her and guilty that she had not protected her.

Dissociative responses in sessions

Dissociative responses are also very common within therapeutic conversations about traumatic material.

Lindsey used dissociative techniques to cope with her traumatic experiences. At first I am sure this happened when she didn't want it to, but over time she became adept at 'switching off' so she 'couldn't be touched by what happened to her'. At the time she came to see me she was a teenager. She attended sessions on her own and never missed a session, but she was rarely 'present'. It took me a while to realise that Lindsey and I were not connecting in her sessions. We were not co-constructing anything. She answered my questions – a performance devoid of feeling and the capacity to evoke change.

I asked her to explain how she did it – this switching off – I also asked her if she could choose to 'stay switched *on*'? Could she help me to understand when she was 'going for the switch' so I could modulate our conversation to ensure she could stay with me.

This is an example of using what Cecchin called curiosity – a 'social constructionist refinement of the therapeutic position of neutrality' (Carr, 2000b, p. 145). Curiosity about 'switching off' opens new conversational territory.

Clients who are still in the grip of their traumatic experiences find their own way of coping with the overwhelming feelings. This is often through external means rather than internal affect regulation. Lindsey's case shows how she used dissociation to deal with her overwhelming feelings – an internal form of flight. This may be more common for people who have been traumatised in situations where they are unable to physically flee. Clients will bring those coping mechanisms literally into the therapy space – knives, violence, drink, switching off.

Conclusion

Working with trauma often produces a 'hole in the mind' that stops people from realistically assessing danger. Creating a context for healing starts within a safe space and is maintained by safe pace and attention to the spoken and unspoken communications arising. Engaging clients in this journey to a better quality of lived experience is essential. It requires the clinician to be resilient and withstand the discomfort produced by confronting and discussing the traumatic experience, daring to consider and introduce other possibilities and begin a dialogue about overwhelming trauma without being overwhelmed in turn.

4

STORIES WE TELL OURSELVES

Introduction

This chapter explores the 'stories we tell ourselves' to deal with the overwhelming nature of traumatic experience. Traumatic narratives are likely to be 'repetitive, vivid, perceptually based, emotion laden and involve a reliving of events in the present' (Brewin in Friedman *et al.*, 2007, p. 123). Therapeutically it is important to introduce difference into these traumatic narratives. This may include different perspectives over time or from other people. More detailed stories with complexity and depth begin the 'migration of identity' (White, 1995) from trauma narrative, which becomes the totality of lived experience, to life stories, where traumatic experience is not constricting identity. This is an essential part of the healing process.

The purpose of the story and general themes from traumatic narratives will be highlighted. These themes include denial, witnessing, minimisation, making choices and forgiveness. Examples of stories told over generations are presented that link the past to the future through the present, as well as those that capture resilience and resistance.

The function of stories

Stories serve many purposes. They can provide a metaphorical encapsulation of particular themes or issues that can be worked through in the therapeutic process (Smith, 2005b). Traumatic experiences often restrict or inhibit the views that people take on their experience by narrowing perspective to 'that which is necessary for survival'. The traumatic narrative often remains a frozen one (Blow and Daniel, 2002). This includes being frozen in time but also devoid of any affective nuances.

'Trauma can efface memories of all that has preceded it ...' (Kassow, 2007, p. 13). In this way it can become shaping of both past and future narratives. Traumatic experience 'cannot be forcefully forgotten, cannot be banished from the history of [our lives], but it can be connected to in a different way' (Flemons, 1991, p. 111). This making of connections, reviewing, renewing and reworking stories of traumatic experience helps to promote healthy and healing stories about adversity.

Naming traumatic experience

Naming and speaking about traumatic experiences is fundamental to processing them – turning them into explicit conscious intentional recollections rather than reliving them through unconscious unintentional remembrances. This telling is part of the healing process (Tomm, 2002). The very nature of traumatic memory often precludes the verbal exposition. Traumatic experience can lead to a life of unwanted remembrances and conscious avoidance. This can be seen as 'forgetting', but until the story can be told without reliving it at the same time, it is difficult to contextualise the traumatic experience within the totality of lived experience. Putting traumatic experiences into words is challenging. 'In the face of horror, language ... simultaneously frustrates and consoles' (Kassow, 2007, p. 7).

Clinical vignette 4.1 is from a family therapy session. The 12-year-old son has been referred to a child and adolescent mental health service by his GP. The boy is described as 'upset and distressed' by recent family events, including the incarceration of his father for domestic violence offences. He attends the session with his mother and two older sisters, 16 and 14 years old. This extract comes early in the session.

This clinical dilemma of naming the traumatic experience and developing a coherent narrative is made more complex by working with families, as seen in Clinical vignette 4.1. Each person's experience of the traumatic event is different. When a parent needs to process their traumatic experience, accessing those memories or stories for their children can make their distress greater and possibly compromise their ability to be the parent their child needs them to be at this time of crisis. Not talking about 'it' can become the family's collective story. This can be intended as protective. The 'crying' in the family session became intolerable and the conversation about 'father's incarceration' became incarcerated itself.

Children need their parents' emotional support if they are to manage overwhelming stress. This is dependent on relational resilience.

CLINICAL VIGNETTE 4.1		
Speaker	**Spoken conversation**	**Clinical reflection**
Clinician	I know there has been some violence in your family. (Nodding by all family members present.)	This information was in the referral letter – it is introduced for transparency and to open up the conversational space for the family story about the domestic violence.
Mum	Carlton's father is in prison. (This is said as matter of fact.)	Using the descriptor Carlton's father highlights one role and also makes less visible another – consider the difference if she had said 'My partner is in prison'.
Carlton	There was lots of shouting and arguing. (Then turning to his mother) Was it worse than that? (There is an exchange of looks between other members of the family – all older and female. They begin to cry. Followed shortly by the boy also crying.)	It seems the boy is using this context to seek more detail about what has happened at home or confirmation about something he knows or suspects.
Mother	I don't want to go into it with him being here.	This is a clear message about pacing; emotional tone and the family's current inability to talk together as a family. Mum is also making a boundary state-ment – taking a generational position about what can be discussed in this context at this point in time. Mum taking control of the content of the session produces a more relaxed atmosphere. Everyone stops crying.

Continued |

CLINICAL VIGNETTE 4.1 *Continued*		
Speaker	**Spoken conversation**	**Clinical reflection**
Clinician	Okay – do you think there is a connection between Carlton's upset at school and his dad going to prison?	Making a connection between what has been presented so far and the referring issue is tentative.
Mum	I think so – he has only been getting into fights at school ever since his father went away. (His sisters remain silent. He begins looking at the floor.)	There is a risk that Carlton will become the problem. Consider his developmental stage – as an adolescent boy in a family where he is the youngest and only boy. It is also interesting to note that 'fights' are the 'symptoms' of Carlton's 'upset'.
Clinician	I understand it is hard for you to talk about what has happened at the moment. Is there someone else in the family that can talk about it with Carlton? To the sisters: Do you talk about it together?	This opens out the discussion to include the sisters and explores the idea of the sibling group's capacity to support each other or to enlist help from extended family members, diluting the 'emotional toxicity' of the verbal recollection of lived experience.

Clinicians need to consider how each individual is connected to the traumatic material? And who is best placed to discuss it? In Clinical vignette 4.1, Carlton's connection to the story of domestic violence in his family is likely to be different to his sister's. He is beginning his journey to manhood and this coincides with his father being imprisoned for violence against his mother. In the clinical work, it would be helpful to consider if there are other men in the family who can be a resource for Carlton at this time.

In working with traumatic stories, clinicians need to be careful not to re-traumatise the client. It is essential in the telling that some aspect of the trauma is resolved or that the client/s leave the session without heightened anxiety and/or with some strategies/self-soothing techniques until the next session. In the absence of this, clients may be tipped into increased flashbacks, heightened arousal and possibly engage in dysfunctional means of affect regulation such as self medicating through drugs and alcohol and/or traumatic re-enactments. This can lead to avoidance of therapy sessions and strengthen ideas that not talking about the trauma (avoidance) is a better strategy because talking about increases anxiety.

False memories

In co-constructing narratives with clients, we need to be mindful of false memories and the clinician's role in possibly creating them. Perhaps this occurs when a clinician hijacks the client's story and fills in gaps or makes connections that the client has not made on their own.

Allow the client to remember their stories themselves, rather than making associative connections for them. When working with families or groups, this may mean waiting until someone is ready, willing and able to share their traumatic experience in a family or group context.

Clients can also hijack narratives – stories they choose to adopt as their own. This process of hijacking becomes more likely where there are 'gains' to be made from doing so. This could be in the form of recognition, compensation or granting of residency. The 'hijacking' can occur as part of the search for identity or in establishing a new identity. Often traumatic experience triggers this course of action.

Take for example the work of Bruno Dossekker who constructed a false identity for himself as a Holocaust survivor and published, under the name of Benjamin Wilkomirski, *Fragments: Memories of a Wartime Childhood* (1995). He claimed that 'he was able to discover his "origins" only with the help of a therapist and detailed research on the victims of Holocaust' (Salecl, 2000). In the ensuing exposé, it became clear that Bruno Dossekker had his own adverse childhood experiences which he superimposed on to his imaginary Holocaust identity. The collapse of the metaphor 'I feel *as if* I were a Holocaust survivor' led to 'I *am* a Holocaust survivor'.

These falsely constructed stories can be described as 'mood in search of reason' (Mollon, 2008). The affective state of the client resonates with the stories of someone else. A need for recognition and collective belonging overrides moral and ethical issues in appropriating the discourse of others.

Developing and evolving narratives

Helping children be realistic about what their parents can provide, as well as helping parents to understand what their children need from them, becomes part of the collaborative process. This interplay needs to be readjusted and reviewed over time, taking into consideration life-cycle events.

Consider the situation for Dawn, another woman who was subjected to domestic violence and stalking by her partner. Her husband and father to her children was convicted many years earlier when her children were much younger – five and seven years old. In therapy her two children – a son now aged 14 and a daughter 16 – have expressed a desire to see their dad, despite a restraining order preventing him from contact with his former partner. Her position of excluding him has to be reviewed in light of her children's age and stage of development. The exclusion of dad from their lives, meant as a protective measure, is now seen by the teenagers, in particular the son, as an extreme reaction on their mother's part. Her son began to challenge her version of events, questioning whether it was really as bad as she said. The wider extended family were divided about how best to proceed, with some members thinking the teenagers should have contact and others thinking it would be too risky. The paternal grandmother attended a session to help consider the situation. In listening to the different stories from the extended family network, including their father's mother, their paternal grandmother, both teenagers decided it was too risky to see their dad but that they could perhaps write to him via their paternal grandmother.

Moving away from an either/or polarity into a both/and loop allows mother's experience of extreme violence to coexist with her son's and daughter's curiosity about their father. This led to conversations about how safety could be maintained if any contact was going to happen. It also meant adding complexity to the story that the children had grown up with about their father. They had, for instance, not been told about his serious mental health problem and protracted periods of hospitalisation. Helping mother to elaborate her story and articulate her reasons for taking what was viewed as such an extreme position was a primary focus of the work. The traumatic nature of the experience meant a story had been developed which had not been modified or changed over time and which minimised the dangerousness of the previous situation.

Using multiple perspectives

Developing multiple perspectives on traumatic experiences facilitates the process of healing. It can be through many media – spoken, written, art, dance. These performance activities can be brought into the family narrative arena. It allows and facilitates the 'as yet unsaid' to begin to emerge in a way that can be tolerated and managed by the system. These creative acts can provide maps for interpreting or making meaning out of the worst experiences. Different approaches and perspectives all contribute to the richness of experience, especially of resilience. It gives shape to 'knowing', which can take many forms. We can think we know; we can know without knowing; we may not know at all but feel we should (Vickers, 2007) – all of these 'nuances of knowing' will be present in clinical work.

A traumatic experience impacts not only on the individual but also on those surrounding them in families and communities. Part of the process of recovery involves opening up discussions about other perspectives on the traumatic event or experience. Often an individual can only see the experience from their own perspective which, because of the overwhelming nature of trauma, is a narrow fragmented perception.

Take kinship carers for example: it can be difficult for them to consider the seriousness of domestic violence. The kinship carers occupy at least two key relational roles simultaneously – parent and grandparent. This can produce role conflict for them. Doing what might be best for their grandchildren may bring them into conflict with their children.

Even when grandparents step in to help or care for grandchildren, they can still find it hard to accept the impact of the adverse childhood experiences on those children. In part this can relate to their own journey to fully comprehend the traumatic situation. And once this has been acknowledged they may question their own actions – Should I have stepped in sooner? Should I have done something differently? What signs did I miss? These conversations going over traumatic events and considering all the options help to process the experience which can happen quickly and can require an individual to make decisions when they don't feel ready or can't fully comprehend what the decision entails over the longer term.

Opening a window on past experiences through family sessions facilitates discussion of the different stories and perspectives in operation at the time, as shown in Clinical vignette 4.2. Leon (14) is cared for by his grandparents. In this session they are discussing how Leon came to live with them. He had lived at home with his mother and father. There was domestic violence and both parents had substance abuse problems. Leon's grandparents were unaware of these issues until Leon was removed from his parents' care and they offered to have him live with them full time.

CLINICAL VIGNETTE 4.2		
Speaker	**Spoken conversation**	**Clinical reflections**
Leon	I remember you having me at weekends – did you?	As the child begins to make sense of their experience, they may seek confirmation of their recollections from significant others. It is important to establish a time line to scaffold life experiences.
Grandad	Yes we had you come and stay with us every weekend. We thought it would give your mum a break.	The purpose of the weekend stays was to help Leon's mother rather than to support Leon *per se*. Whereas caring for Leon now is a shift to privileging his needs for safety and security over his mother's need for support.
Leon	I liked coming but I always felt sad when you took me home. I didn't understand why you did that.	Leon in sharing his feelings about being returned, provides an opportunity for his grandparents to explain their actions and make reparation.
Grandma	It breaks my heart hearing you say that ... We didn't know what was going on ... we knew things were a bit difficult but we had no idea how bad it was.	Domestic violence and substance abuse are often denied and kept secret. Articulating this mismatch in perception is important.
Clinician	To grandparents: I think it is important for Leon to know that you were not aware of how violent it was at home when you took him back. Or that his parents were taking drugs.	Leon needs to know his grandparents were not knowingly returning him to the violence and drug abuse.
Leon	I thought you knew ... I wanted you to know.	This allows discussion on what prevented them from talking to each other at the time about the violence and drugs.

Speaker	Spoken conversation	Clinical reflections
Grandma	I feel so bad about it now Leon. Your granddad and I are sorry. We were so focused on your mum and trying to help her out we didn't see it from your perspective.	This explanation underlines that they were privileging their role as parents over grand-parents.
Leon	You still do it now though – you take her side and make excuses for her.	Leon now picks up a pattern – his experience that they still sometimes put his mum first.

Clinical vignette 4.2 shows the multiple perspectives operating simultaneously in a family session. Practicalities can take over, and the opportunity to review the traumatic events that led to a dramatic change in family life can be avoided or not considered important. There can also be misunderstandings about situations. In vignette 4.2 there is an opportunity for Leon and his grandparents to consider the 'perspective of other'. It led to an important discussion of pattern that Leon comments on – 'You take her side and make excuses for her'. This reflection was unexpected and prompted his grandparents to reconsider some of their behaviours and consider greater clarity of role when dealing with their daughter and grandchildren.

Stories of denial

When an individual has been traumatised they can oscillate between positions of denial and repression on the one hand and intrusive memories, re-enactment and flashbacks on the other. This oscillation can become sufficiently violent as to cause catastrophic disconnections (like suicide or psychotic breaks with reality). Moving to a position of active forgetting – of knowing when and what we need to know – takes someone from a frozen narrative perspective to one where context shapes the necessary knowing.

Anna in her therapy also kept a journal which we discussed from time to time. In one excerpt she wrote:

Is all this relevant? I feel it is to me. It helps me to make sense or not of why I must break the chain.

Systemic psychotherapy helps people understand that their behaviours, feelings, ways of being are the result of many experiences, some passed through generations. It opens 'an alternative territory of identities (plural mine)' (White, 2005a). It helps an individual to view their experience through a number of contextual varifocal lenses.

Stories of denial are very common. They can facilitate day-to-day functioning in adverse conditions by supporting a view that 'it is not so bad really'. While this may be helpful in the short term, the minimisation of the traumatic experience often produces symptomatic behaviours which can manifest as physical or psychological distress.

These stories of denial can be based on misinterpretation or reinterpretation of experiences in a way that allays anxiety or disquiet. This 'premature cognitive certainty' may establish or maintain a comfortable position within the family or wider social system. However, it may mean remaining in a traumatic situation for longer or failing to act on behalf of others in traumatic situations. Domestic violence is a good example of traumatic family experience that is covered up within families and communities.

Stories of witnessing

Clinical vignette 4.3 comes from a kinship care support programme. Grandmothers caring for their children's children are discussing how they allowed themselves to believe 'it was not so bad really' for their children and their grandchildren.

For Chrissie and Jean the reality of the domestic violence their daughters were being subjected to resulted in the removal of the children and care of them being taken over by the grandmothers. The story of miscarriages hides a sinister aspect of domestic violence. Both daughters remained with their violent partners, going on to have other children following the removal of the ones being cared for by their mothers. What stories must they have told themselves to believe this was the best way forward? Consider how this choice to remain with a violent partner will impact on the children being cared for by relatives.

These stories the grandmothers shared demonstrate a collective denial within extended families and communities. For example the story of miscarriage becomes a vehicle to hide an ugly consequence of domestic violence. It allowed the culture of secrecy and the abdication

CLINICAL VIGNETTE 4.3		
Speaker	Spoken conversation	Clinical reflection
Chrissie	I kept hoping she would find someone nice to settle down with but it was like each guy was worse than the one before.	The stories of optimism and hope sometimes blind people to what is really happening. They witness what they believe.
Jean	I know what you mean; I just put my worst fears to the back of my mind. I thought he might be hitting her but I kept telling myself it wasn't my business.	Acknowledging the worst may require actions. 'It's not my business' becomes a rationalisation for non-intervention.
Clinician	When did it become 'your business'?	This question opens up the discussion within the group about what prompted them to change their views and intervene. Often it will be a peak episode that penetrates the overly optimistic view – the witnessing of something dissonant – so incongruent with the dominant narrative of optimism it produces a dramatic shift in perception. Using Jean's construction of 'my business' helps lead into the area of responsibility and respectful boundaries.
Chrissie	Well we already had Michelle [granddaughter] living with us. She [Chrissie's daughter] seemed to be getting on alright with the new man in her life. She had two more children and then social services became involved. There was	The intervention by a wider system – social services – acts as a trigger. This can enable family members to step forward more confidently but it can also strengthen family loyalty. Cultural stories about the interface between public and private will come into play. 'Snitching', 'grassing', 'telling *Continued*

Speaker	Spoken conversation	Clinical reflection
	violence between them and he had a heroin problem. I feel bad now because I left Anna and Daniel with her and they had to live through all that. But you know before that I kinda knew. She miscarried at six months ... this was before Anna came along. I asked her if everything was all right ... you know a mother's intuition.	tales' are often very negative discourses. The denial of 'mother's intuition' can prompt feelings of guilt.
Jean	You saying that reminds me that Louise [her daughter] miscarried before Lily was born. He'd kicked her in the stomach.	The group context allows other untold stories to be shared.
Clinician	Do you think with the benefit of hind sight these miscarriages were part of the domestic violence?	Both women seem to have considered this a possibility.
Jean	I know it was. We didn't say anything though. We never spoke about it. She stayed with him. It made me sick at the funeral with him carrying on ...	The untold story, had it been told, may have threatened the relationship her daughter was so committed to keeping.
Chrissie	It's murder really isn't it. I couldn't bring myself to say or even see it at the time. But in my heart I knew he'd caused the miscarriage. He threw her down the stairs. She was six months – showing and all.	Silencing is active. It involves concealing something known and felt but not worded.

CLINICAL VIGNETTE 4.3 *Continued*

of responsibility for actions to continue. Many parents convince themselves the children do not know. However children often do. The children can develop hypervigilance and are likely to be sensitive to any signs of pending parental arguments.

Stories of minimisation

In Clinical vignette 4.3, the issue of pregnancy and its impact on the domestic violence is raised by the grandmothers. This led them to consider the impact of domestic violence for those unborn children. They can be primed to anxious responding whilst still in utero.

Bev in her family sessions repeatedly stated:

> You have the wrong idea – it wasn't domestic violence. He wasn't physically violent with me. It was more an attitude of mind – a form of psychological controlling.

While this may be true, she then went on to describe the night when he pulled her by her ankles off the settee in front of the children. Later in therapy she discussed years of marital rape. Like denial, forgetting and minimisation can have a protective function. While still in the traumatic situation, it is perhaps necessary as a form of survival. It can also be functional in the longer term. Angela, one of the Irish care survivors, shares this memory in her recollections:

> I have a friend who has no recollection whatsoever of anything that happened to her in the convent. One assumes that is her way of dealing with it. Yet I recall her standing in front of the altar on a daily basis with her wet sheet around her shoulders – a pissy shroud. She doesn't even recall bed wetting.

Angela has an understanding that this is her friend's way of coping but for some survivors of a collective trauma such as abuses within residential care, this absence of memory can be seen as a betrayal or a form of discrediting the other's story.

Consideration needs to be given to the issue of survivor guilt which is present in some trauma stories. Witnessing the trauma of another (as in domestic violence for children or the abuse of other children, as is the case for institutional abuse) can cause a traumatic response for the witness. For many survivors, there is the shameful feeling of relief that they were not the subject of the abusive behaviour.

These positions of denial, minimisation and forgetting can become a way to 'sidestep' the traumatic memory. Unfortunately, trauma has a way of seeping out into day-to-day living often when least expected.

By not naming traumatic experience individuals can continue to live their preferred narrative of self. For Chrissie and Jean this may mean being respectful mothers, trying to find the right balance between interfering and allowing their daughters independence, or for Bev, trying to maintain a 'good father' for her children and not wanting to see herself as a victim of domestic violence. In each of these examples a tension arises when the preferred story no longer fits the lived experience. This dissonance often brings people into therapy.

Stories of forgiveness

The following clinical example focuses on developing a different perspective of the traumatic narrative. It involves a young girl referred to CAMHS for work on her traumatic experiences in Kosovo. Emmanuela was particularly disturbed by an incident that involved a soldier throwing a rock at her. She dreamt about this incident repeatedly.

Dream work is not often mentioned in systemic practice despite its obvious story potential. Dreams, like poems, often present difficult material in contracted metaphorical clarity. They can provide the systemic practitioner with a 'creative grammar' (Lang and McAdam, 1997, p. 7) that can be elaborated into new realities.

Emmanuela was encouraged to become the observer and amanuensis to her dreams. Traumatic experiences are often 'relived' through night terrors, often unremembered, which can be worked on to become nightmares recalled by the client and then progress to dreams – removing the negative affect associated with nightmares. We worked through the layers/levels of fearful awareness. When she first attended she was not aware of her night terrors; these were reported by her parents. This helpful recounting by her parents allowed Emmanuela to take control of her dreams – reclaiming them – and begin to use the material from the dream to consider her experience.

Over time she became aware of the recurring dream narrative. She recorded what fragments she could remember and we tracked each new piece of information.

Diary entry 18 August:
The soldier threw a stone at my forehead and then he said something but I don't know what it was because I didn't understand it.

This was the first time in her dreams that the soldier had spoken to her. We began talking about this in therapy. I encouraged her to tell me what she would like to happen in the dream conversation. She began by drawing a picture of the recurring image from the dream. She had drawn pictures of him, his head turned away from her. The picture is of the 'peak episode' – the soldier [an identity] throwing a stone [an act] at her as a child [a developmental stage]. Her lack of understanding is multilevelled. She didn't understand him literally, as they didn't speak the same language, but also metaphorically, because his conduct is against her own code of conduct even within the context of war.

> Diary entry 28 August:
> I saw a man that was a soldier and I said 'Why are you doing this? Why are you throwing a stone at me?'

This entry demonstrates the changing perspective as the soldier has now become a 'man that was a soldier'. It shows the importance of closely analysing text (in this case) for signs of change. In our sessions it becomes clear they cannot speak to each other because they do not speak the same language. They need to 'co-construct' a shared language (Gergen, 2001; Shotter, 1993).

As her dreams continue, the soldier begins not only to speak to her, but also to turn and face her. Her diary records the repetitive nature of the dream but also the slight but significant changes. She repeatedly asks 'Why?' [Pse]. The dream occurs in her mother tongue, Albanian.

We begin to explore what she wants or thinks he might say. She wrote a range of alternatives in English:

> Sorry I didn't know what I was doing.
> Can you forgive me?
> I must have made your life hell and I'm really sorry.
> Or if he's cruel and I say 'Can you say sorry in a way that you mean it?' He might say 'Why should I say sorry when I know you will not forgive me.'

The dreams carry on but now the soldier has become a man, in part his humanity restored, he is saying he is sorry and turning around to face her. Forgiveness is clearly a theme for Emmanuela. Forgiveness frequently arises as an issue within trauma work especially when the traumatic experience is relational, as in the case of sexual abuse or domestic violence.

However, this is not the theme I pick. I ask her to think about herself in this dream. 'Are you still 10 years old? How long are you going to go on giving him a chance? Are you ever going to walk away?'

These questions were intended to help focus Emmanuela on alternative ways of being and repositioning herself in the story. If she sees forgiveness as her only path to recovery, she may feel hopeless about resolving the situation. She is struggling with the soldier taking responsibility and apologising for his actions. He may never do that. She also has some doubts about offering forgiveness if his apology is not heartfelt.

The repetitive nature of the dream and her request for answers could be seen to demonstrate how a person can start off from a position of strength (confronting a perpetrator for example) and move to a position of weakness by continuing in the interaction when desisting rather than persisting might be more appropriate. This shows how resilience in one context might become a weakness in another.

Her desire for answers to her questions keeps her in the relationship. This underlines that systemically forgiveness must be seen as interactional. How do apologies and forgiveness manifest themselves in interactional ways and across the life cycle? (Mullet and Girard, 2000). These themes of forgiveness and reparation often arise in wider systemic contexts.

Believing in the centrality of forgiveness for healing to occur can 'effectively [place] control of survivor's healing in the hands of the perpetrator of abuse. If forgiveness is to be given without admission of guilt or repentance, it asks the survivor to display a truly superhuman capacity for understanding' (Jones, 2007, p. 151).

Stories to rationalise difficult choices

When a difficult choice needs to be made, a narrative can be developed to explain those decisions. In a traumatic circumstance, someone may have to make a decision quickly that can have long and enduring consequences. They may have to come back and consider what they did and how they justified their actions. It often begins with a story they tell themselves.

Caitlin abandoned her baby with a note. In her note, she talked of needing to 'hide the child from his father' and how if he knew about him 'he would take you away ... That's why I have to do this ... There's no one else who could help us'. The baby, Jacob, was reunited with his mother. In her therapy, the note she left became a focus for discussion.

The reality of her situation bore no resemblance to the story she had created. Jacob's father had no idea Caitlin was pregnant. Far from being on her own, Caitlin came from a large, loving, extended family that did support her when it came to light that she had left Jacob to be found and brought up by someone else. Caitlin needed a story that made her act seem a heroic, loving sacrifice rather than an act of fear or shame. The story she created made it possible for her to abandon Jacob. In being reunited with Jacob, Caitlin had to confront her shame and fear.

In discussing the untold story of fear and shame, Caitlin had to share an unwanted and traumatic experience with her family. This experience was something she had tried to conceal. Along with the experience, she concealed her pregnancy, the birth and subsequently the baby. Had she kept her baby, she would have to tell a story she wasn't able or ready to tell at the time. When she was reunited with her baby, it became a necessary part of the reunification that she try and explain to her family what she had been unable to do previously. Her parents talked of their hurt that she couldn't talk with them and had to go through her ordeal alone. They also felt protective of her and admired her bravery in coming forward. They supported her through her reunification programme.

By allowing other participants into the co-construction of healing stories, a richer discourse is promoted. Leon's conversation with his grandparents – telling them of his confusion and anger at being returned to the family violence – broke through the denial and minimisation of the experience by his grandparents. This allowed them to apologise for letting him down and also enabled them to talk of their future hopes for him. Caitlin was able to tell her parents about the traumatic event that led to her pregnancy. She was able to talk of her fear and shame and they were able to show her understanding and support. Because traumatic events underpin these examples, these conversations had not taken place spontaneously. Sometimes connections are not made between traumatic past events and current crises. Multiple perspectives can help to confirm and reframe the experience.

Stories over generations – linking past to future

Family stories have a special place in fostering resilience. They reflect the dimension of family time and are especially important. Thinking over generations can help individuals manage and survive traumatic experiences at the time as well as bringing different levels of meaning to experience, dependent on generational position. Family stories are effectively 'palimpsests onto which each generation inscribes its own impressions and removes some of the marks of earlier generations' (Aston and Rowley, 1974).

Claudia Poblete's grandmother, in describing her experience of searching for her grandchild, child of her 'disappeared' child, high-lighted the different generational positions a common event has. The traumatic event between them – the disappeared child/parent – will be viewed and experienced from different generational positions. Finding her granddaughter was the end of the grandmother's search, and simultaneously it was the beginning of a 'traumatic journey of discovery' for her granddaughter (Qassim, 2007).

Emilia Dowling and Gill Gorell Barnes (1999) highlighted the different positions family members occupy when divorce and separation occur. Not everyone travels through this process on the same timeline. One part of the marital partnership may have started 'leaving' the relationship much earlier than the other. Children can be unaware of their parents' difficulties and be taken by surprise when they are told of impending separations. This multiple timeline perspective is also true for shared traumatic experience.

When working with families where trauma is an issue, there will be different generational perspectives active in the therapeutic context. While trauma may focus attention on the past, it can also shape the future. This can be in the form of expectations for poor future outcomes or repetitions of the traumatic experience. Many mothers of boys who have witnessed domestic violence are concerned that their sons will be violent towards future partners. This can become a 'self-fulfilling prophecy'. Rarely is the spectre of trauma – the ghost at the banquet – mentioned, yet everyone can be organised by it.

Trauma time is discontinuous. In a strange way it brings the past to the present in an unhelpful way – a reliving that prevents living in the present and shapes the future for repetitive replays. It becomes a flat confluence of time with a predictable outcome, rather than a lively interplay with many potential outcomes.

The following clinical example shows how family stories over generations are a rich source of meaning. Niamh had been in care since she was six years old following experiences of sexual abuse. She was referred with a view to her being rehabilitated home to her mother and mother's new partner. She was now eight years old. In preparing for this she was asked for stories of her mother. What could she remember about her mother? There were two striking stories she recalled.

The first was that her mother was a terrible cook and burnt food all the time. The second was that her mother had no hair. I shared these stories with Maire, her mother. She burst out laughing and confirmed that she was still a terrible cook. This became a good connection between mother and daughter. It confirmed Niamh's remembrances but also gave them a shared history that could be humorous rather than emotionally heavy.

The story of hair was interesting. I was puzzled by Niamh's description of her mother as having no hair. Maire confirmed that as a younger woman and at the time she had full care of Niamh she was in her 'punk' phase. She had shaved off all her hair. She went on to describe her punk phase as a rebellion against her strongly Catholic mother. She said her mother was obsessed by her daughter's hair and kept it long. Shaving it all off had been an act of defiance towards her mother. She had never considered that her daughter might see this as scary or strange.

I asked why she thought her mother was so obsessed by hair. Maire described her mother's childhood experiences in an orphanage where her long hair was cut off and kept short in an unflattering way. Long hair was seen to be a sign of personal vanity and a source of sinful pride. We then traced how hair had become a connecting theme for mothers and daughters. Maire's mother wanting her daughter to take pride in her long hair was reparative for her, who had been forced as a child to keep her hair short. Maire had never thought that her mother's 'act of defiance' was in allowing Maire to have long hair.

When Niamh and her mother, Maire, met in therapy, they both immediately remarked on each other's hair. They discussed and played with hair – putting it up, brushing it out, putting it up again – for much of the session.

We absorb messages contained within stories passed down through our families. We can track those relational patterns over time and generation (Selvini *et al.*, 1980). In this case, hair and femininity were powerfully intertwined, like a plait. For Niamh's grandmother, her beautiful hair was seen as threatening and potentially a source of sinful vanity by a wider social system; for Niamh's mother, allowed and encouraged as a little girl growing up to enjoy her long hair, it became a symbol of parental oppression and was shaved off; for her daughter this absence of hair became a reminder of a woman she didn't remember very well who had failed to protect her. Hair became the link between generations and a source of reconnection.

Here is another example that demonstrates how layers of meaning and context collapse into family stories. Anna's family had a culture of secrecy which she described in her therapy journal. She sometimes wrote to me thanking me for 'listening'. This describes the importance of 'other' in making sense of experience. The very act of writing her thoughts and feelings down became symbolic.

I've always been afraid to write any of my thoughts down, as if afraid of seeing my words confirm real traumas which have happened to me. ... I want to keep the words in, hidden away so deep, never to hear, let alone see.

This journal entry eloquently describes the power of language, written and spoken – its power to confirm, affirm and transform. For children, it is their parents who help them give language to their lives. When this fails to happen, the languaging of experience and the potential to make meaning needs to occur elsewhere. Sometimes this is in therapy. However, as the next journal entry shows, the inter-session reflections are often just as important – the expansion of ideas into wider life experience.

I had a revelation sitting here on my bed, you said something a while ago to me, that I was a psychological orphan...

'Psychological orphan' was not a term that she had produced herself, but in describing her parents to me, both alcoholics, I used it to convey having parents who were not psychologically available to her. The term psychological orphan resonated for her both in describing her own experiences as a child but also in her struggle as a mother herself.

This term 'psychological orphan' helped Anna understand why she struggled to be a 'good enough mother' to her own daughters. The parental models she had to draw upon from her lived experience were absent. The clinician reflecting and co-constructing a narrative of experience can facilitate the emergence of new identities. Sometimes clinicians provide a metaphor that the client takes up as their own. Perhaps this needs to be acknowledged more. Meanings should not be imposed but offered tentatively.

Anna went on to describe seeing her daughter

filled with self-loathing. A trait I know so well. This is the legacy I passed on to my children. I have failed them badly because I was not equipped emotionally or otherwise to give them what they needed. I'm reliving my own abuse through them and I feel terrified.

Often when clients write to me, I respond in kind. I wrote back to Anna.

It is strange how writing your thoughts down does make it seem as though what you are writing is more real.

The acknowledgement of hearing or reading something previously unworded is fundamentally important in co-creating stories that will enhance rather than diminish people's identities (Fredman, 2004, p. 4; Smith, 2005b).

My letter goes on:

> sometimes when women are confronted with the sexual abuse of their own children, it reawakens feelings from past experiences that may have been forgotten. I am not surprised that you can't sleep or that you are reliving your own childhood suffering. ... you are working on being able to separate what your daughters need from you and what you need for yourself.

This addresses the multiple identities vying for attention. Anna as mother to her daughters wants to give them a reparative experience but her own experience of victimisation and lack of reparation from her mother is making it hard for her to know how to manage. Helping Anna find the courage and the strength to be the strong mother she wanted to be formed part of the healing narrative.

I encouraged her to think of the big picture:

> look back through the generations of your family ... The depth of your pain is not just your own, it is the pain of your mother, the pain of your grandmother, the pain of your father – all these people who tried to make better lives for themselves but failed in different ways ... It isn't just your struggle but the struggle of your family over generations, trying to come to terms with things that don't make sense. Small things and big things – things that involved sexual abuse within the family and activities beyond the control of any family, like civil unrest in Hungary.

This is part of establishing a collective discourse and introducing a multiplicity of views. Helping to contextualise and moving between the multiple frames of experience, allows a richness to develop. It can promote curiosity and consideration of hidden areas of strength that can be celebrated, nurtured and developed.

Stories of resilience and resistance

Some stories embed exceptions – the seeds of resistance and resilience in the face of overwhelming odds. These stories may need to be embellished. In considering Anna's family story, this led to a discussion about how her family managed to leave Hungary at a time when this was difficult.

At the family level, Anna noted that her father, despite being an alcoholic, never hit the children; that her step dad, although involved in criminal activities, did not abuse the children or her mum; and that his criminal activities ensured a degree of economic stability for the family. This opens up the possibility of complexity and richness in considering family roles and relationships, moving away from a monochromatic description of abusive childhood experiences. It also helps her to focus on family strengths despite adversity. In reviewing what seems like a devastated life, encouragement to find what should be salvaged, nurtured and developed becomes transformative.

Helping Anna to remember the bigger picture enabled her to find in her repertoire of selves the mother she had wanted when she had been a child. She began to enact this identity. She supported and stood by her daughter, encouraging her to talk about her experience; asking for forgiveness for not preventing it from happening and working towards building a strong mother–daughter relationship in the present and for future generations.

Many parents experience secondary post traumatic stress when confronted with the traumatic experiences of their child. This can range from an episode of life-threatening illness to other types of traumatic events. For Anna, her daughter's experience of sexual abuse traumatised her as she had tried to be so vigilant and protective. It activated her own traumatic memories of her childhood. It could be that Anna remained in a hypervigilant state regarding sexual abuse as a consequence of her experiences, but it may also be that the additional stressor of her daughter's abuse reawakened her own fears and cast doubt on her identity as a protective mother.

Identifying identity

Stories over the life cycle and within families shape personal identity. These stories can contain themes from previous unspoken traumatic events.

Daniel was the youngest of six children. The only boy in his family. He was removed, with his siblings, when he was three years old. There were high levels of violence from his father toward his mother and all of the children. Everyone felt convinced that Daniel had been protected and that his early removal from his family of origin meant that 'He didn't remember anything. He was too young.'

He was referred to therapy by his foster mother at age 10. He was seen as very sexualised and in need of high levels of supervision.

Daniel 'who didn't remember anything', described in detail his father's belt – the one he used to beat his sisters. He also described and graphically represented his worst fear – that he was going to be like his father. As the only boy in a family with an abusive father, stories of masculinity were limited and restricted.

He represented himself at the beginning of therapy as half devil and half angel. He described this as his father (devil) in him (angel). At the end of his therapy he produced another picture – a separate father and son. His father's actions having been acknowledged and discussed with Daniel allowed a separation to take place and for Daniel to explore other discourses of masculinity.

This kind of discussion will be revisited over the life course as Daniel reconsiders aspects of his own identity as a male; as a partner; as a father. The templates for masculinities will move towards complexity rather than remain collapsed around violence. It is important to introduce the idea of fluid identities that change in response to different life cycle issues.

In helping Daniel articulate his worries – 'the things he didn't know' – he developed distinctive voices including that of his foster parent. Often he enacted conversations between the voice of his father and his foster father – the former telling him to rob and the latter telling him not to. Helping Daniel and his foster father recognise these voices led to encouragement for Daniel to create his own preferred identity. This allowed both of them (Daniel and his foster father) to open up new territories of identity. His foster parent began to see his influence as a father figure, which encouraged a sense of entitlement to 'parent' Daniel. Daniel was given permission to draw on alternative stories to construct a preferred identity. The idea of Daniel 'turning into his father' lost some of its destabilising power.

One can escape into a different identity that brings completely new affective associations or redefine/reclaim an identity that has been tarnished through traumatic experience.

Identity is very shaping. Sometimes in the search for a new identity an individual can assume radical transformations that can be very disturbing for family and friends. For example, Naomi Shragai (2007) described how her father, 'a Jewish camp survivor who had lost his parents in the Holocaust, who participated in the building of the state of Israel suddenly turn[ing] into the Christian mythological figure of Santa Claus?'

We need to recognise the necessity for multiple identities and see the fluidity of those identities as part of healthy resilient living.

Conclusion

Telling stories activates the cerebral cortex, engaging more of the brain in the experience, and broadens associative connections to the experience. Stories are soothing and narrative acts as a process of integration. A coherent narrative about a traumatic experience is indicative of a 'good recovery'. It suggests that the experience is no longer taking over and being relived. It may still be painful and emotional to recall but it is seen as in the past. Survival is not just physical but also psychological. It represents the reunification of the mind, body and soul, often separated in the traumatic deluge.

5

WORKING SYSTEMICALLY WITH PTSD SYMPTOMS

Introduction

This chapter will focus on the major symptoms of PTSD – those distressing, disturbing behaviours and feelings that often bring people to therapy. It will provide a systemic understanding of the most common symptoms associated with post traumatic stress disorders: flashbacks, intrusive thoughts, avoidance, nightmares/terrors, re-enactments, hyperarousal , hypervigilance and catastrophic disconnection.

Currently, clinical guidelines for PTSD in the UK (NICE, 2005) recommend 'watchful waiting' for children and young people in the first instance and then, where symptoms persist for more than three months, eight to twelve sessions of trauma-focused cognitive behaviour therapy. There is clear guidance that 'debriefing' or single interventions following a traumatic event should not be routinely done. Pharmacological approaches are discussed for adults. For symptoms deemed to be mild and acute, it is considered best to let time pass and reassess. For moderate or severe symptoms of at least one month's duration, trauma-focused interventions are recommended. It is suggested that the interventions are offered on a one-to-one basis with the exception of children and young people, where families should be involved. Systemic clinicians need to consider this advice and how to incorporate it into their practice. Early intervention following a traumatic event is more successful.

A meta-analysis of factors that increase risk for the development of PTSD (Ozer *et al.*, 2003; Trickey, 2009; Trickey and Black, 2000) highlighted the absence of social support and current-life stresses as highly significant. Both of these are context-related, suggesting and emphasising the importance of working systemically in this field. The intersection of the past and the present produces narratives that constrain or broaden the quality of lived experience.

Systemic therapists and symptoms

Historically, within systemic thinking, strategic therapists like Jay Haley focused more on symptomatic behaviours. Symptoms were seen as performing an important relational function and a form of communication. They were seen as metaphorical encapsulations of the 'not yet said' and as solutions to an often unacknowledged issue. The field of systemic psychotherapy moved away from what is now seen as '**problem-saturated stories**' or a focus on 'symptoms'. Moving too quickly away from, or not paying enough attention to, distressing or disturbing aspects of lived experience can ultimately lead to an unsatisfactory therapeutic experience for the client, whose symptomatic behaviour is often what brought them to therapy in the first place. Not attending to those 'symptoms', or failing to consider the impact of trauma, may put clients at risk by not addressing specific safety issues or the distress that may be stirred up by 'talking about it'.

'Reframing' the symptomatic behaviours as previously helpful but no longer necessary suggests that a significant change in context has not been noticed or that other solutions may be more effective in dealing with the current dilemma. What presents in the clinical setting are those 'solutions' that are unsuccessful in providing a *satisfactory way of being* for the individual or for significant others within their immediate context. It may be that a failure to understand what the system is communicating results because the clinician has not understood fully the context that made it meaningful (Cronen and Pearce, 1980). This can include safeguarding issues, drug and alcohol problems or domestic violence, where secrecy and shame are an integral part of the situation or traumatic experience, which is avoided, denied or disconnected in conversation. Not speaking of traumatic experiences becomes a way of 'linguistically deferring reality' (Masters, 2012).

Traumatic experience, especially chronic exposure, can curtail new learning and almost certainly recalibrates responses to future stressors (MacFarlane, 1997; Van Der Kolk *et al.*, 1996). It is thought that recurrent exposure to fearful stimuli encourages individuals to react to ambiguous situations *as if* they are threatening. There appears to be a failure to differentiate between contexts. Over time this simultaneously lowers and heightens the threshold for fearful responses. Someone with PTSD is not fearful of situations where they should be scared and, paradoxically, is too fearful of situations that they shouldn't be. It is a failure to discriminate and to distinguish what signs are significant (Bateson, 1973, p. 389).

Symptoms can be seen as metaphors based on similarity (condensations) and metonymies based on contiguity (displacements) of psychic distress. One can see systemic therapy as focused more on the condensation of meaning and much less on the displacement of meaning. The trauma becomes not known by its own name – it remains nameless, unspoken and sometimes unworded, but enacted, embodied and relived repeatedly.

Common symptoms associated with PTSD

While fear is often the most frequent emotional response, many people cope through numbed responsiveness or aggression; the fight or flight continuum. It is important to be open minded about the emotional responses someone may have to a traumatic event – while fear is one of the most common, shame, betrayal, guilt and rage may be present. Different emotional responses may emerge at different stages in the life cycle for the individual. Family members, or those who experienced the same traumatic experience, will all react in unique, individual ways. This can make family or group sessions more complicated to manage.

These feelings can be mapped on to lived experience. Threat often leads to fear, provocation to anger and scorn to shame. These actions (threatening behaviours; provocations; denigration/scorn) are often present in traumatic experiences. Sometimes a significant aspect of the traumatic narrative will be omitted, often linked to an affective response that is considered to be unacceptable.

This example is from work with Michelle, an eight-year-old child referred following the murder of her mother by her father six years earlier when she was only two. She has been living in a kinship care placement. She was asked what she wanted help with. Her first item was:

I feel ashamed because my mum is dead and I didn't know her.

This came as a complete surprise to everyone. The idea that Michelle felt shame was not something they had considered. The family had been prepared for sadness and fear but not shame. Shame can block access to emotional information (Andrews *et al.*, 2000; Mollon, 2008, p. 112). The family, in their own shock and grief, had stopped talking about Michelle's mum. This request from Michelle opened up the possibility of 'getting to know her mum' through stories shared by family members. This celebration of her life balanced what had become the dominant story – her traumatic death.

Symptoms that are specific to traumatic experiences often take over and become the dominant story. This can include intrusive thoughts, avoidance of reminders, nightmares and flashbacks. Importantly these symptoms focus on the traumatic experience itself. The content of these experiences is trauma specific (McNally, 2009). For children this is often manifested as repetitive play or re-enactment of the trauma. Adults can repetitively re-enact their traumatic experiences and not always as the victim. This can be common when working with adult offenders who re-enact their victim experiences by victimising others. In an attempt to master the traumatic experience, they assume the role of the perpetrator. This narrative distortion can take over other more healthy ways of being.

We need to be mindful of a developmental perspective in relation to symptomatology across the life cycle. For example, the processing of traumatic material may be something that is attended to in the later stages of life as part of looking back over life experiences. Traumatic memories can be triggered by life-cycle events. For example, becoming a parent may activate memories of childhood traumas.

Interventions aimed at increasing resilience

A trauma-based intervention needs to deal not only with the traumatic narrative but also with increasing the repertoire of self-soothing skills the client can use to help deal with the expressed emotions and more detailed remembrances of the trauma experience. De-escalation and affect regulation are key components of many trauma-based interventions (Bradley, 2000).

Advances in developmental neurobiology give strong support for the importance of experience-dependent relational interventions to rehabilitate infants exposed to prolonged relational trauma (Schore, 2003a, b). Making these complex ideas accessible to clients involves developing a common language that can generate different approaches to some of the challenging behaviours evident in traumatised individuals.

The self-soothing programme is a group work intervention designed for primary caregivers which focuses on affect-regulation techniques by introducing brain-directed interventions. All the children being cared for have experienced adverse childhood experiences. Many would qualify for a diagnostic label of PTSD. The programme focuses on different aspects of brain function, including the senses – sight, sound, smell, touch – breathing exercises, relaxation and physical exercise. There is a strong psycho-educational component to the programme. Each module has an experiential aspect, with an expectation that the primary caregiver teaches the learned techniques to the child they care for. The programme, which has developed over the years, encourages primary caregivers to be actively involved in affect regulation for themselves to reduce the risk of secondary PTSD and for the children they care for, many of whom have attachment difficulties and do not consider adults to be resources. In this way it uses systemic ideas around relationship to strengthen and support recovery from adversity.

The importance of context, especially the family, on good therapeutic outcomes is well recognised. Systems-based approaches focus on a coordinated approach, embracing the multiple contexts children live in.

One kinship caregiver in the self-soothing programme was describing her granddaughter in a temper tantrum – throwing herself about in a rage. Her inner conversation consisted of recognising that the 'iguana brain' had taken over. This term 'iguana brain' emerged in the programme as a way of explaining midbrain driven behaviours.

In considering that the child was in an 'iguana brain' state, she felt compassion for the child – not anger or irritation. She used some of the self-soothing techniques she had learned on the programme. The effect on the child was immediate.

This example shows how the caregiver's perception of the child's behaviour had changed as a consequence of information she had been given, this allowed her to access different parental strategies to deal with the situation. It also shows that it may be helpful 'to go outside the theory in order to accept and use, temporarily, another one' (Bertrando, 2007, p. 109) – in this case an intervention based on neurological skills.

Identifying 'iguana brain' has been helpful in family sessions, allowing other family members to lend their frontal lobes to the 'temporarily dispossessed' family member. This reflects the complexity of work where ethically one needs to consider a range of interventions and abandon notions of theoretical purism.

Increasing the repertoire of self to include for example 'checklists for signs of social and psychological resistance' (Denborough, 2008) is likely to deliver a better 'return on resource investments given that these skills are more likely to be employed and to induce beneficial effects on a regular basis, rather than being "dusted off" and used only under extraordinarily stressful circumstances' (Layne *et al.*, 2007). This type of approach, increasing self-soothing techniques, fits with a life-cycle model.

If traumatic experiences and resiliencies travel along a lifelong continuum as two intertwined strands, then at certain points in life an individual may be more or less susceptible to stories dominated by traumatic experiences or resiliencies.

Flashbacks and intrusive thoughts

Flashbacks are an involuntary repeated memory of a strong emotional nature. They are one of the most commonly reported symptoms of PTSD. These repeated remembrances are often intrusive; occurring seemingly out of the blue for no apparent reason. They also disrupt the continuity of time, as they tend to disorient the individual because the strong emotional component of the memory is re-experienced rather than remembered. This brings the past uncomfortably into the present.

Charlotte Delbo (2010) grapples with the idea of the twisting narratives of trauma and resilience when she refers to *'memoire ordinaire'* and *'memoire profonde'*.

> Between the two is a skin ... which memoire profonde sometimes pierces. The skin covering the memory of Auschwitz is tough. Sometimes however it cracks and gives back its contents (quoted in Vulliamy, 2010).

This is a striking description of the process being put forward. Symptoms 'pop up' through the skin of memory as a reminder that there is something that still needs attention.

The following is an excerpt from a letter sent by a young boy, who had been abused in his family of origin, to his clinician. He had been frustrated by his inability to describe what he was experiencing and what he wanted help with. He was encouraged to put it into writing. This is what he produced and brought to his next session.

> When I am angry I have flashes of violence like someone walks towards another person and then they hit that person and blood goes flying out of the person then it goes blank. When I try and think of good things, it all ends up as someone hurt. ...

This suggests that when he becomes angry for any reason, the internal affective state activates visual images of violence. The neural pathways to violent imagery are better developed than the pathways to 'thinking of good things'. This 'thinking of good things' could be developed by imagining and talking about 'good things' repeatedly.

> Whenever I think of my mum, it is a picture of me in a cold bath with her standing on the left side and my step dad on the right side – laughing together while I am scared, frightened and worried because I don't know what's going on. ...

This second excerpt shows that 'thinking of mum' also triggers a vivid traumatic picture and associated feelings of fear and anxiety.

This 14-year-old boy is clearly describing flashbacks. They are in part triggered by affective states – like when he gets angry – and trace back to a peak episode where he is helpless and confused by his mother's actions. He is finding it hard to change how he thinks because the affective states cut off his associative cortex and the traumatic memories hijack his current lived experience. 'Good things end up as someone hurt' is a relational pattern. Helping him to consider exceptions and develop those narratives, as well as specific self-soothing techniques to override the anxious responses, are essential to begin the process of him living his preferred narrative.

Steven (13) was referred because of inappropriate behaviour. There was a history of domestic violence in his family when he was less than five years old. His mother has a new partner.

He attended his first session with his mother. He was able to talk about and externalise his problems – how 'bad Steven' took over at times. His mother talked of how this reminded her of her ex-partner. At the beginning of the session she was not able to name her ex-partner except as 'HIM'. Clinical vignette 5.1 comes midsession.

Steven's mother is describing a traumatic flashback activated by her son's behaviour. Her hypersensitivity means she responds to Steven's aggression *as if he were* her domestically violent husband. For her the 'as if' disappears, emphasised by her stating 'I mean it really is HIM'. At that point of high fearful arousal, she can no longer discriminate between her son and her violent ex-partner. She is not living in present time but in trauma time. Clearly, in highly charged emotional situations with her son, aspects of the boy's behaviour – his anger, his physical appearance – act as triggers for the traumatic memories from her relationship with his father.

Although Steven has been distressed by his father's domestic violence

CLINICAL VIGNETTE 5.1		
Speaker	Spoken conversation	Clinical reflection
Steven	I get angry and hit out.	The child has produced an affective state and an action. This connection can be explored and potential other actions developed.
Mother	He's so like HIM when he does that.	The child's behaviour becomes a flashback for the mother.
Clinician	What do you mean?	This is to encourage Mother to use narrative to help remain in the here and now.
Mother	He looks like HIM; sounds like HIM ...	Instead she becomes more absorbed and overwhelmed by the flashback to her ex-partner.
Clinician	Is that hard for you both?	This is meant to punctuate or disrupt her traumatic recalling.
Mother	It brings back reminders. At those times he becomes HIM I can't see Steven anymore I only see HIM.	It is unsuccessful for Mother, who carries on. This gives the clinician an insight into how it feels for Steven.
	Steven cries.	It produces a different affective state for Steven – one of sadness.
Mother	I mean it really is HIM.	His mother is so locked into her past traumatic experience, she cannot attend to her son's distress.

he is not showing evidence of being traumatised by it. This is not the case for his mother. When she relives her past experiences the narrative part of her brain is switched off. This switching-off is currently beyond her control because she is still triggered into her past experience. When triggered, she is not in the present and she is not remembering what has happened. She is *reliving* what happened.

From Steven's point of view this must be frightening. He is not trying to be like his father – he is being himself – but is perceived by his mother as his father. While this experience for mother and son may be languaged; it is not primarily a 'languaged experience' – it is activated by feelings or affective states. When his mother is confronted by her angry teenage son, she no longer responds to him as his mother but becomes a victim of domestic violence. The situation does not de-escalate but becomes frightening and dangerous for both of them. This pattern of interaction between mothers and sons where domestic violence has been a feature is often apparent as the young boy begins to mature into manhood. This life-cycle transition can trigger memories from the past for the mother that have remained unprocessed while her son was still a boy.

These examples show the complex interplay between family members who have shared a traumatic experience and how powerful flashbacks can be.

Clinical vignette 5.2, involving Tommy (10), relates to intrusive thoughts when he feels anxious. Tommy has had some therapy before. At this session he is attending with his mother.

CLINICAL VIGNETTE 5.2		
Speaker	**Spoken conversation**	**Clinical reflection**
Clinician	Your mum has told me you get really anxious and sometimes you get really bad thoughts ... is that right?	Sharing what has been previously shared is helpful in promoting transparency and ensuring the focus of intervention is clear and mutual.
Tommy	Nods yes	
Clinician	What was helpful about your previous therapy?	Checking out previous interventions tries to minimise repetition and doing more of the same. It is also an attempt to engage Tommy.
Tommy	Taught me to think about other things and about my breathing ...	This clarifies what Tommy 'took' from his previous therapy.
Clinician	And if you were thinking about your breathing right now; how is it?	This is an invitation to show competence and build on previous skills. *Continued*

CLINICAL VIGNETTE 5.2 *Continued*		
Speaker	**Spoken conversation**	**Clinical reflection**
Tommy	I'm relaxed.	This is helpful as a baseline.
Mother	He's always checking his breathing. He does panic. He's checking all the time. He just feels he's going to stop breathing.	Mother's comment 'he's always checking' seems dissonant with Tommy's previous comment about being relaxed. She is also talking about him and possibly for him. A hypothesis about whether she had to do this for a long time arises. Is there an event that increased her maternal anxiety?
Clinician	(To Tommy) Do you have any ideas about what starts these bad thoughts up?	By asking Tommy, this tests the level of separation between him and his mother. Is he able to think for himself?
Tommy	Being on my own mostly; sometimes with mum and dad [who live separately] but never with my sister.	Tommy provides a relational context for his bad thoughts.
Clinician	Maybe you should be with her all the time then? [laughter]	Humour is used to keep the emotional tone of the session 'light'. It also draws attention to the exception.
Mother	He won't discuss it with his dad. At his dad's, he phones me twice to tell me he's had thoughts. I tell him to go and do something like play on the computer.	Mother provides more relational information. Tommy seems strongly connected to his mother and more emotionally distant from his father.
Clinician	To Tommy Does that calm you down?	Checking out strategies that work.
Tommy	Yes	He is lapsing back into monosyllabic answers.
Clinician	She's pretty neat your mum – a good crisis centre – but it would be difficult to spend the rest of your life getting your mum to calm you down.	Reframing the close connection as helpful now but potentially problematic later highlights life-cycle issues.

This example shows how Tommy's mother acts as an affect regulator for him. He is unable to calm himself down. This has increasingly become an issue for Tommy and his mother. At a time when developmentally he should be able to manage his own anxious feelings, he still requires his mother to do so. This suggests that something is preventing Tommy and his mother from moving through this transitional stage successfully. The dramatic nature of his fear (that he will stop breathing) makes it hard for his mother to ignore. This suggests there is a traumatic narrative as yet untold between them.

Tommy has given a clue about which relationships trigger his anxiety in describing the exception – he does not experience panic with his sister. When separated from his mother, often at his father's home, he begins to experience overwhelming anxiety. This is an opportunity to explore the exceptions in terms of context and not just relationship.

The example uses humour to diffuse tension within the session. The use of humour needs to be respectful and facilitate the capacity to be self-reflective (Cecchin *et al.*, 1994, p. 9). Humour often arises by seeing connections between things that don't naturally go together. The odd juxtaposition frees the mind to make new connections and not be overly constrained by context. When anxious, clients can become stuck in their thinking. Humour can allow them to become unstuck.

In the examples given, feelings or affective states trigger 'symptomatic' behaviours, including dissociative responses. Traumatic experiences can stop individuals from accessing certain identities at critical times. It can limit the response repertoire to the survival tactics of midbrain-driven behaviours.

Avoidance

Avoidance forms a significant part of what happens after a traumatic experience. It is a strongly held belief that not thinking or talking about 'it' is the best way to manage the overwhelming feelings that come up. This avoidance often prevents people from entering therapy or leads to them abruptly terminating therapy once they have started.

Michelle (described earlier in this chapter whose mother had been murdered by her father), when asked about her worries produced the following list:

1. I feel ashamed because my mum is dead and I didn't know her. I wish I knew my mum.
2. I have visions. I know what's going to happen. My visions are mostly at night time. *I don't want to talk about this* (author's emphasis).
3. I have trouble reading, writing and spelling.

She is clearly letting me know that she is not able to discuss point two on her list. While we can work easily on points one and three, point two will take considerably longer as she is actively indicating this is not something she wishes to discuss.

Using nonverbal methods for processing trauma can be very helpful. This can include writing it down without sharing it out loud, or using some of the specific treatment techniques that have been shown to be effective in processing traumatic material, such as the tapping sequence in **emotional freedom techniques (EFT)** or the eye movement desensitisation reprocessing (EMDR) protocol, and then revisiting the written story. This allows children to process traumatic material in 'private'. **Externalisation** through the use of bad memory box can also be helpful. Families can devise rituals for keeping 'bad memories' in the right place.

It is important not to underestimate the value of the presence of someone else when processing traumatic material. It helps if the 'other' is calm, assumes a 'posture of tranquillity' (Fredman, 2004) and is prepared to be a witness to the process. This is in part why family work around traumatic material needs to be done with sub-systems, as the telling of a shared traumatic experience can activate traumatic responses in other family members and, rather than producing a positive transformation, heightens and sensitises everyone to negative effects associated with the traumatic experience.

The 'dialectic of trauma' is the 'conflict between silence and the desire to proclaim' (Herman, 1997). Treading this delicate line is challenging. Clinicians may not need to know the details of what needs to be dealt with when acting as a facilitator or catalyst for change.

Consideration needs to be given to working around avoidance – bringing the unspeakable into the realm of conversation. This is where imagination, dream, play and drawing can all help to open up discussion safely. There may also be a need to consider the benefits of not talking about a traumatic experience. Asking clients how they knew they needed to discuss their traumatic experience can provide useful reflections.

Nightmares and night terrors

Nightmares and night terrors often form a significant part of the clinical presentation. It is often the symptom the client is least aware of. This emphasises the importance of discussing symptomatic behaviours with significant others. Many adult survivors report no sleep difficulties but their partners indicate otherwise, often giving detailed descriptions of night terrors.

Pavor nocturnus, another name for night terrors, occurs at a different stage of the sleep process than nightmares, which occur during rapid eye movement (REM) sleep. Clients will have no recollection of night terrors but can recount their nightmares. Night terrors can sometimes involve getting up and walking about, often in a fearful or anxious state. Parents and partners witness these, which is often very distressing.

Leyla, a 14-year-old girl, was referred due to night terrors. The night terrors were interfering with her day-to-day living. She was having four or five episodes a night which meant she was often too tired to go to school in the morning. Her night terrors involved getting up out of bed in an agitated fearful state and checking rooms in the house for fires. Her parents could persuade her back to bed but after a while she would begin over again.

Not being able to get on with developmentally appropriate tasks is one of the indicators that a specific treatment intervention is needed. Positioning Leyla's parents as key players in her treatment was essential. They recorded the number of episodes she experienced. When she awoke at night, they talked to her, reassuring her it was safe and returning her to her bed. Over time the night terrors became nightmares as Leyla became more able to recall them. This phase of her treatment was accompanied by being told when awake what she had been trying to do when asleep – bringing the distressing material into daylight. This involved discussing the fire that had devastated the family home.

Witnessing the traumatic re-enactments of significant others, but especially children, is a risk factor for developing secondary post traumatic stress.

Rituals can also help with night terrors and re-enactments. Jack (six) began having nightmares involving his dad, who had been violent, getting into his foster home. On a home visit Jack, his foster dad and I did a 'safety tour' of the house. His foster dad reassured him about the safety he provided for his family. This included physical things like locks on doors and windows, but also vigilance. He talked with Jack about how Jack's father was not allowed to come into this house unless invited. This led to a discussion about how Jack's dad was turning up uninvited in his dreams. The discussion about these nocturnal intrusions helped break the secrecy. It allowed Jack's foster parents, primarily his foster father, to provide an alternative story about the role of fathers in families. The 'safety inspections' were carried on until Jack felt reassured about his safety and his father stopped 'visiting uninvited'.

Re-enactments

Tracking patterns over time can also reveal traumatic re-enactments. Like a genogram that tracks family patterns over generations, a timeline of significant events can track patterns over time.

Helen was working to get her children back from care. She had been in an alcohol recovery programme and was nine months sober. As part of a group work programme, she was asked to reflect on her family of origin stories of drink (her family cultural set up). She recalled the story of her mother drinking when her parents split up (her relational template). She described this as losing two parents – her father who left and her mother who was emotionally unavailable.

The trauma timeline exercise also involves tracking resilience. By interweaving the two themes of trauma and resilience, it is clear that at certain points 'relapses' can be predicted because of the congruence with previous traumatic dates or circumstances. These can act as triggers to activate the trauma line. Specific attention needs to be focused on those times when relapse seems more likely. Often these are connected to time – time of day, day of week, time of year. It is as if the body's clock remembers and prepares for the traumatic event (Van der Kolk, 1994). The following example demonstrates this.

Helen was due to have unsupervised contact with her children for the first time in 18 months. Instead of being happy, she felt scared and anxious. She was showing behaviours that suggested a relapse was imminent – these included not getting up, not caring for herself – behaviours associated in the past with her drinking identity. She didn't understand why her feelings were so at odds with what was happening. When she was asked what else was happening in her life, she identified a major loss – the death of a friend. This triggered feelings of loss in Helen that resonated with those she experienced when her partner left her. These two losses are contiguous events though they are separated in time by two years because they evoke similar affective states.

Helen was asked to focus on the loss of her partner and how this had impacted on her relationship with her children. This was to connect the theme of loss with the current issue of contact with her children and to explore the hypothesis that feelings of loss overwhelm Helen's parenting capacity. Losing her partner had led to an escalation in Helen's drinking which in turn led to the removal of her children.

Thinking about the impact of traumatic loss in Helen's life raised the possibility that her current emotional state has been triggered by a memory. The affective state of feeling anxious and afraid is also likely to trigger a re-enactment of her previous coping strategy – drinking. Her behaviours and mood were totally at odds with the present circumstances in her life where she had been drink-free for nine months and managed to earn the right to see her children unsupervised – a goal she had been working towards.

Table 5.1 shows a two year time frame going back from the current dilemma. This is how Helen mapped out her timeline. She selected her own significant events. Subordinated stories of Helen's strength, resilience and resistance are also being tracked. The text highlights events that contribute to Helen's stories of herself as succeeding on her road to recovery. Helen started her trauma line with her partner leaving her. This was significant as it suggested her identity as a partner was one of the most significant roles in her life. She described him as 'the love of her life'. In considering the loss of him and recognising that June 200Z represents two years since they split Helen began to cry. 'I'm still not over him ... When I see the children, I will see him in them'. Her enforced separation from him [and the children] has enabled her to avoid dealing with her loss. For her, losing the 'love of your life' is strongly connected with losing the will to live. This is also a repetition of a pattern from her family of origin, when her mother began drinking after her father left the marriage.

Helen raises another important point in relational trauma – the way in which physical resemblances can act as triggers. In her example she states: 'I will see him in them'.

Cynthia Owen (2010) raises this issue when considering why her mother was particularly abusive towards her. 'I was the only child that looked like her. I had her red hair and green eyes, while all the others were dark. I don't know if that was some kind of trigger'.

Many women who conceive through rape or sexual abuse can find it impossible to bond with the baby because the physical characteristics of the child, often the eyes, trigger memories of the traumatic experience. Given the importance of eye gaze in the attachment process, this bonding difficulty is not surprising.

TABLE 5.1

Traumatic events and self defeating behaviours	Acts of strength, resilience and determination	Clinical comments
June 200X Partner leaves her. Her drinking increases.		Stories of addiction almost always contain minimisation. Helen's relationship with drink predates her relationship with her partner and children. It becomes her primary relationship.
December 200X Car crash. Contact with children ceases due to her drinking. Spends Christmas drunk.	5 December 200X Oliver born	The birth of her child was seen as a celebration. However given what has been described in the June, this clearly suggests she has been drinking during her pregnancy. Oliver currently in care may need to be screened for foetal alcohol spectrum disorders (FASD) – an as yet untold story.
March 200Y Oliver removed.		Helen sees her partner as responsible for Oliver's removal. This strengthens her story as a victim.
November 200Y Septicaemia – almost dies.	November 200Y Period of sobriety.	Life and death in close proximity is a reflexion of the close relationship between trauma and resilience. The first building block of a 'sober identity' is contiguous with a near-death experience.

Traumatic events and self defeating behaviours	Acts of strength, resilience and determination	Clinical comments
November 200Y Moves to hostel for homeless.		Helen identified this as rock bottom for her. She is on a 12 steps programme.
	17 November 200Y First day of sobriety – makes a commitment to remain sober.	This time frame has a cluster of events both good and bad. November will be a critical month for Helen.
	December 200Y First sober Christmas – no contact with children.	The new identity as sober is dominant for a steady period.
	January to May 200Z In the programme. Continuous sobriety	
June 200Z Programme friend dies.		A confluence of events – one good and bad – occur in June. Themes of loss and abandonment are rekindled.
	June 200Z First unsupervised contact with children due to occur.	

For Helen, the June to November period represents a downward spiral of escalating depression and suicidal drinking, preoccupation with self and focus away from being a parent. A rehabilitation plan running over these months is likely to fail as Helen is not yet out of her downward spiral. The six month window between June and November her body remembers as slowly dying. These patterns and time frames are sometimes not understood or recognised as significant when planning interventions.

Helen starting her timeline with her relationship breaking down points to this important aspect of her identity. While the court intervention focuses on her being a parent to her children, her unresolved grief about her lost marital relationship is intervening and could potentially sabotage the rehabilitation programme.

Tracking the intertwining stories of resistance and resilience allows her to create a vision of her future that strengthens these stories. Helen needs to learn from her life and find the support she needs to create a different future. Being a mother means a lot to Helen. She had always dreamed of having a large family. The car crash in December 200X was the incident that provoked her partner and father to her children to stop Helen's contact. This would be considered a peak episode. When this incident was discussed Helen told the following story:

> I was at my sister's house. I had been drinking but only a few cans. He said he was coming over and I wanted to spare the children having to hear another heated argument between us. All I could think of was to get away – take the children to my mum's. I got in my car and drove off. The car crashed. No one was badly hurt luckily but the police came and I was breathalysed and found over the limit. This was all he needed to stop me from seeing the children.

Within this story, Helen's other identity as a protective mother is hidden. Her *intention* was protective but drinking had impaired her judgement. Had she walked to her mother's house or taken a cab – it may have delayed or possibly prevented her having contact suspended. Helping to highlight this aspect of Helen's identity is vital at this point in her journey to becoming the mother she wants to be for her children. This might enable her to remain on the path of resilience, recovery and resistance.

Therapy is often challenging because it encourages remembering what the client wants to forget. In the remembering, as in this timeline exercise, there are often aspects of self that are hidden and need to be reclaimed. It is important to highlight the intertwining of competing narratives of self. It is difficult for 'parents under state surveillance, [to] persevere with us in a dialectical enquiry that [brings] forth a redeemed future from events of failure' (Byrne and McCarthy, 2007, p. 47).

Table 5.2 shows another example. Donna was referred to a counselling service following her conviction for child abandonment. In her therapy Donna was asked to construct a timeline starting two years prior to her being identified as the mother of the abandoned baby.

TABLE 5.2

Traumatic events and self-defeating behaviours	Acts of strength, resilience and determination	Clinical comments
	November 198A Donna making a go of her relationship with her first real love.	
June198B Her real love confesses he doesn't want to have any children and pressurises her to have a termination.	June 198B Donna discovers she is pregnant.	This late termination was very traumatic for Donna. It was against all of her beliefs. She had never spoken about this. She felt guilty and shameful about this experience.
June 198B Relationship ends.		Despite acquiescing to her partner's wishes the relationship ended. This made Donna feel even worse about the termination.
November 198B Donna is date raped.		Clearly another traumatic event. This has also never been spoken about.
February 198C First inkling she is pregnant from the rape.		Donna never considered she might become pregnant from being raped. She pushed this 'inkling' to the back of her mind and did not disclose her pregnancy to anyone.
July 198C Gives birth and abandons baby.	Donna gave birth at home on her own. She washed the baby. Dressed it and wrapped it up to keep it warm. It is found almost immediately.	These small acts of kindness to the baby are significant.

TABLE 5.2 *Continued*

Traumatic events and self-defeating behaviours	Acts of strength, resilience and determination	Clinical comments
November 198C Donna identified as mother of abandoned baby.	Pleads guilty and engages in counselling.	This suggests she is prepared to take responsibility for her actions.

In working on this time line, curiosity about her late termination was connected to the question: in what context might abandoning a newborn be seen as a protective act?

Like the termination, she kept the rape and subsequent pregnancy secret. She felt overwhelmed by shame and coped with both traumatic events by denial. Secrets of this nature can be deemed 'booby trapped heirlooms' (Imber Black, 1998), storing up distress that often comes out unexpectedly. For Donna abandoning the baby, although better than having another termination in her mind, did not succeed in deleting the traumatic experiences from her mind. It is likely Donna went through the latter part of her pregnancy and the birth in a dissociative state. The recognition that Donna was the baby's mother began a process of discovery and recovery for both the mother and child.

These two examples of trauma timelines give a clear illustration of the twisted nature of traumatic and resilient actions or intentions. In both cases, competing identities shape the decisions and hide the more hopeful resilient identities both women possess. Both were deemed 'bad parents' and their own feelings of guilt for what they had done stifled other stories which demonstrated they possessed a 'good enough' parent within them. These examples show how Helen's and Donna's therapeutic 'disclosures exceeded the bounds of a confessional narrative to become a redemptive act[s]' (Byrne and McCarthy, 2007, p. 44). Treatment work focusing on thickening those narratives of hope and resilience enabled them to reclaim their roles as good enough parents.

Hyperarousal and hypervigilance

Hyperarousal and hypervigilance are often triggered by reminders of the traumatic experience. This is why thinking about the experience from the client's point of view, including the developmental stage they were in at the time the traumatic experience occurred, is helpful. Many trau-

matised individuals are not able to articulate what triggers their traumatic memories. They may not recognise these agitated states as unnat-
ural because they have lived this way for so long.

Angela who spent time in an Irish orphanage more than 60 years ago
captures this in her comment.

> I'm not sure what hypervigilance is. If it's anything to do with being
> extra vigilant then I definitely fall into that category. I am very much
> aware of things that go on around me. I am always on the lookout
> just waiting for something to happen and I always expect the worst
> rather than anything good happening. ... I respond to things too
> quickly. I often get hold of the wrong end of the stick and somehow
> think people are getting at me.

Claudia Poblete, 'abducted' at eight months from her disappeared
parents in Argentina and placed with 'adoptive' parents (Qassim, 2007),
describes this highly anxious state she has always lived with without
understanding why. She is reviewing this from the perspective of an
adult who now knows the secret about what happened to her as a baby.
Her adoptive parents never told her she was adopted nor about the
circumstances of her adoption.

In thinking about her life as a child she provided this reflection:

> I was very frightened as a child. ... I was terrified of being left alone.
> Sometimes I would go to my [adoptive] parents' bed to check if they
> were still breathing. Now I understand why I had this fear, this feel-
> ing of abandonment.

Had Claudia's grandmother not gone in search of her granddaughter,
Claudia may never have understood her underlying sense of anxiety
and separation fears.

This highlights the importance of asking significant others (partners,
parents or primary caregivers) about behaviours and any triggering
events or situations. The individual may not be able to recognise or
assess their own situation because it is habitual for them.

Self-soothing or affect regulation is an integral part of the healing
process in recovering from trauma. Learning to turn off the hyperarousal and hypervigilance aspect of mind is difficult as it serves a
protective function – to preserve safety, to watch out for and avert any
future dangers. Helping others in the significant network to understand
the positive function of hyperarousal and hypervigilance opens up the
possibility of different responses to the associated behaviours. It also

encourages them to be involved with establishing a new sense of safety, especially important when the trauma is relational in nature.

Catastrophic disconnection: self-harm, psychosis and suicide attempts

Maintaining such high levels of vigilance and arousal is physically and mentally exhausting. This can lead to serious depression and fatigue affecting 'mind and body; psyche and soma'. Chronic exposure to stressors, especially at developmentally sensitive stages of life, can lead to lasting changes in the neural circuitry (Schore, 2002). This in turn can impact on physical health by compromising the immune system functioning because of exposure to stress-related neurotransmitters. Unregulated somatic experiences triggered by reminders of traumatic events are signs of chronic physiological arousal, often at the root of recurring post traumatic symptoms that bring the client into therapy (Ogden and Minton, 2000).

There is also evidence for a link between psychosis and trauma. Morrison *et al.* (2003, p. 331) considered three pathways in examining the links between psychosis and traumatic experience. These were: 'Can psychosis cause PTSD, can trauma cause psychosis and could psychosis and PTSD both be part of a spectrum of responses to a traumatic event?' Their overview found support for a positive answer to all three questions and led to an integrative approach to clinical management.

For the client it is exhausting to live an interrupted life – one where time is constantly going back on itself suddenly, unexpectedly and space also suddenly and unexpectedly seems to collapse.

The antithesis of what Susan Sontag suggests is the purpose of time and space. '... Time exists in order that everything doesn't happen all at once ... and space exists so that it doesn't all happen to you' (Rieff, 2007). When everything happens all at once and only involves the individual, cutting them off from their relational world, it is overwhelming. It can produce 'catastrophic disconnections'. This includes significant breaks from relating to others through extreme behaviours such as self harm, psychotic breaks and suicide attempts. There is evidence to suggest that exposure to traumatic events increases suicidal thoughts and actions (Gradus *et al.*, 2010).

More often it is the negative overwhelming nature of experience that presents clinically. These catastrophic disconnections to traumatic exposure are not discussed in detail other than to raise this possibility.

Management of these potentially dangerous responses requires close monitoring, individual attention and regular review.

Suicide attempts can appear to happen out of the blue. With children and young people there is often an impulsive quality to their suicidal behaviours. It is important to pay attention to the intention of behaviours including, and especially, life-threatening ones.

Self-harm and suicide attempts can occur in dissociated states connected to traumatic experiences. It can be helpful for family members to consider what role (if any) traumatic events may have played in the retreat from life or act of self-harm. Feeling you were going to die at the time of the trauma is a key factor in the development of a PTSD. It is often followed by a sense of a foreshortened future. Angela, now in her 70s, captures this in her reflections:

> You know when I was in my teens I always thought I would be dead by the time I was twenty, then it was thirty, and I used to pray to God to let me live till I was at least forty.

Angela lived with this sense of impending doom virtually the whole of her adult life.

Conclusion

In reviewing the most common symptoms of PTSD, there is considerable scope for systemic interventions. This can involve a recognition of symptoms as 'solutions'; focusing on affect regulation within systems; recognising the importance of flashbacks, night terrors and re-enactments as encapsulated memory of traumatic experience.

Doing this work requires the clinician to deal with avoidance and to look for patterns over time. It requires a strong focus on hope and an acceptance that the past sometimes needs recognition before it can be relegated to its proper time and place.

PART 3

The Practice Neighbourhood

6

WORKING WITH FAMILY, FRIENDS AND COMMUNITY

Introduction

This chapter explores the impact of a traumatic event on the wider systems of family, friends and community networks and how to make best use of them in therapy. It begins with the concept of disclosure, where an individual chooses to share their traumatic experience publicly, and moves to consider discourses in families, communities and wider systems. It touches on the friction produced by different contexts and how these multiple contexts shape and are shaped by a traumatic experience.

Public and private disclosure

The consequences of sharing are often unexpected. If one member of a family has had a traumatic experience it can be felt by all members. For example Turner and Renell's book (1995) *When Daddy Came Home: How Family Life Changed for Ever in 1945* serves as a reminder that the man who returned after the war was almost certainly very different from the one who left. Exposure to war combat is considered one of the top four causes of PTSD (McCrone *et al.*, 2003). Often, personal war experiences are not shared within the immediate family context, making survivors' groups and networks very important resources.

There are many similar books and increasing public awareness about the after-effects of war on service families and civilians. Exposure to combat increases the lifetime incidence of a PTSD from between 1 and 9 per cent to almost 20 per cent.

This high incidence for PTSD is also reported for young adults living in inner cities (see http://www.trauma-pages.com/ [accessed 6 August 2012]). Such a shocking finding underscores the extreme stress many communities endure on a daily basis. Members of these communities are less likely to present to mainstream mental health services and more likely to respond to local community initiatives.

When whole communities are subjected to traumatic experiences, as in war or punitive political policies, the social fabric is damaged. This can lead to traumatised communities. This is but one example of the ripple effects of traumatic experience. Treatment interventions that focus on individuals may deal with specific symptoms but are unlikely to address the impact of trauma on wider systems like family and community.

Living with someone who has a PTSD can increase the likelihood of developing secondary PTSD. The constant exposure to their volatile and emotional lability, irritability, inability to relax and generally depressed outlook impacts significantly on those closest to them. Additionally there may be serious sleep disruption, including night terrors and night-mares. The close proximity, significant relationship and length of exposure make this experience more toxic for family members, often partners.

Working with wider systems, such as groups who share a similar experience, schools, and communities, maximises the resources the group possesses. This support helps to increase psychological resilience and understanding of the experience. Many family members may not realise a family member is suffering with a PTSD. They may try and play down the feelings and the experience in the belief that this will help. Many have been specifically advised not to discuss the traumatic events. This was once considered the most appropriate treatment for 'shell shock' (Rivers, 1918). Many still subscribe to such a view.

All conversations about self constitute a disclosure, as aspects of self and lived experience become visible within the relationship. Disclosure in the UK has become strongly associated with legal procedures, which unfortunately inhibit and distort the expression of lived experience – especially traumatic experience, which until processed inhabits an emotional nonlinear universe of basic survival.

The *intention of disclosure* is worth considering. From a therapeutic point of view, disclosure is part of the process of acknowledgement. Acknowledgement promotes 'a vividness of a specified reality' (Tomm and Govier, 2007, p. 140). Acknowledgement requires a relationship – a speaker and a listener – to confirm what has been expressed. However, the positions occupied by both within a wider cultural context need to be considered, as well as the meaning given to 'being listened to'. Conversation can be viewed as a form of action rather than merely representative (Fredman, 2004, p. 30). In conversation with the other, a shared meaning can be developed that facilitates understandings of and actions with each other (Lyotard, 1984).

The *context of disclosures* also needs close attention. During an assessment interview with a young girl (10), her social worker and grandparents, who care for her, were also present. The focus of the discussion was how best to help her now that she wasn't living with her mum and dad.

After the introductory preamble, the young girl was asked if she knew why she had been asked to attend. 'Yes' she said 'it's about the S, E, X (spelt out)'. The social worker and grandparents were stunned and silent at this information. The child went on to give a detailed story about what had happened to her and why she was glad she no longer lived at home.

This example demonstrates the multiple contexts represented in the consulting room. For her social worker this constituted a disclosure that would require further investigation. For her grandparents this disclosure was shocking and shaming as the sex involved other family members. For the girl it was a discourse representing something disturbing she wanted to talk about and which she considered to be the reason why she wasn't living with her parents and why she had attended the appointment.

Acknowledgement

A foster mother asked for help from a CAMH service with her foster daughter. Eloise, her foster daughter, had a moderate learning difficulty. This manifested as very concrete thinking. Eloise had been complaining to her foster mother – 'You're not listening to me'. Her foster mother ensured that she listened to Eloise, and always repeated back what she heard Eloise say. In trying to understand what was upsetting her it became clear that for Eloise her foster mother 'not listening' occurred when her foster mother did not agree with her. Eloise articulated this as 'not being listened to'.

Eloise has touched on a very difficult issue. There is rarely only one version of events. For Eloise, who is fostered with a younger sibling, her version of events is often very different from her sister's. While this is in part developmentally appropriate, it also touched on family of origin scripts, where her younger sister was 'protected' in a favoured child position. Eloise, despite now being in a safe context and different family, remained hypervigilant for any situations that she considered evidence of favouritism. Eloise perceived 'neutrality' as deeply unfair. Her intention in raising the issue of 'not being listened to' was to point out injustice as she perceived it. Eloise is demonstrating a dilemma: 'if my perspective cannot be understood (by agreeing that it is the way I see it) then I may not exist'. She still needs external confirmation of internal perceptions. In part she needed her past lived experience of 'not being listened to' to be acknowledged.

Helping her foster mother understand the existential and emotional complexity presented by Eloise linked to her traumatic experiences as the 'invisible' one, allowed for different parental strategies to emerge.

Family perspectives on shared traumatic experience

Within the family context, parents can feel a burden for not having prevented a trauma or believing their actions have exposed their child/children to traumatic events. Sometimes they can deny the impact of their behaviour on their children as part of avoiding shared traumatic experiences. A traumatic event will be perceived through different generational lenses (parents, partners, children, siblings) over the life course. Each of these lenses creates new meanings and understandings of experience.

Many of the case examples in this book illustrate the conflict that comes from occupying multiple generational positions simultaneously. This can include the mother of a child who has been sexually abused by her partner (Smith, 1994); a grandparent caring for and bringing up her children's children; or a parent reminded of their childhood abuse when their child is born.

Clinical vignette 6.1 comes from a family therapy session with birth parents of a child who no longer lives with them. The boy, now 10, has been in care since he was three following a physical injury which resulted in his father being convicted. His mother still lives with his father and together they are parenting a younger sister. There has been a longstanding history of domestic violence. Mother suffered with postnatal depression after her son was born. Both parents have had problems with alcohol. Difficulties have arisen in the contact they have with their son, which has included 'play fighting'. Recently their son has refused to see them.

Many parents are confronted with their own traumatic childhood experiences when they become parents themselves. In the vignette, father sees himself as a child in his son. His experience of being

CLINICAL VIGNETTE 6.1		
Speaker	**Spoken conversation**	**Clinical reflection**
Father	I just don't know why he doesn't want to see us (belligerent tone).	Both parents are preparing to be confrontational. This comes across in their tone. Father recognises his son is making a choice not to see them but is unable to consider why this might be so.
Mother	I think it is his foster mum keeping us from seeing him (blaming tone).	Mother is putting the intention onto the foster mother. This allows her to believe her son does want to see them and is not exercising his own choice.
Clinician	Perhaps it would help if you think about it from your child's point of view. Can you remember back to why he came into care?	This question is to assess the parent's empathy and ability to see events from the other's perspective. There is also a connection to the point where the parent/child relationship became disrupted.
Mother	It's all your fault (looking at father).	This is the second time mother has blamed someone else. This raises the hypothesis that she perhaps feels guilty about something she did but has yet to acknowledge.
Father	It is all my fault. I hit him.	Father's acceptance of blame lacks any real remorse. He seems accustomed to taking the blame. This raises ideas about how long this habit 'taking the blame' has been around for him.
Clinician	Do you think he remembers that? Do you think he might think about that when he sees you? (Both	This is an attempt to push them to consider their son's point of view and to discuss the issue of 'play fighting' at some stage.
		Continued

	CLINICAL VIGNETTE 6.1 *Continued*	
Speaker	**Spoken conversation**	**Clinical reflection**
	parents look down). I know when I have met with him, he does still talk about it and is very curious about what happened (said gently).	The silence feels like a silence of acceptance and perhaps shame which opens the door for confirmation that the boy does still talk and think about the traumatic incident.
Father	I did hit him. I admit it. When I see him now though he still pushes my buttons. It's like he winds me up on purpose ... and it's like seeing me ... when I was his age ...	Father repeats his story and elaborates, indicating that the boy still provokes anger in him. He gives his son intentionality and offers a personal reflection that he is reminded of himself as a child.
Clinician	What else do you think he might remember from his time with you?	This is to see if the early childhood experience can be spoken about in more detail and not just collapsed into 'I hit him'.
Mother	I didn't want him – even before he was hit there was something not right about him.	This disclosure is unexpected and painful to hear.
Father	I didn't want him either.	In this feeling of not wanting their son, the parents are united. As they are successfully parenting a girl, gender issues seem to be significant.
Clinician	Has that feeling changed for either of you?	It is seven years since they relinquished this child.
	Silence from both of them.	This is curious – they do not want him but they want him to want to see them. What does the refusal to have contact mean to them as parents? It seems to be experienced as defiance by the father and fake by the mother. This idea is not shared with them.

Speaker	Spoken conversation	Clinical reflection
Clinician	Maybe the two of you weren't ready to be parents yet?	This is a reframe to keep the conversation open and help the parents move to a position of taking more appropriate responsibility for what has happened.

unwanted, difficult and unmanageable is re-experienced. His affective response to this witnessing makes it difficult for him to access aspects of his adult identities and to be the father he wants to be, the father he did not have. This striving to 'be who we want to be' is played out repeatedly over the life cycle. If traumatic experience is involved it can impede the development of new identities or shape them in an unhelpful way.

Involving others in treatment

If a child has had a previous traumatic experience it can make parents over protective. In the next example the father is hypersensitive to issues of protection for his children because of his perceived failure in the past.

Mr Smith was referred for counselling following an episode at his daughter's primary school. His daughter told him she was being bullied. He went to speak to the teachers but felt they were not taking him seriously. His daughter continued being bullied. Mr Smith decided to take the situation into his own hands and confronted his daughter's bullies. The other parents complained about this and Mr Smith received a written warning from the school and was told not to pick his daughter up. Mr Smith ruminated on this and became very distressed and depressed. This precipitated the referral.

In therapy a number of significant issues arose. English was not Mr Smith's first language. He and his family were seeking asylum in the UK having left their country following war and having been victims of persecution. The episode at school had powerful resonances for him with the experiences in his previous home country. He said he felt helpless and a failure for not protecting his family. When his daughter complained about the bullying at school, he felt he should protect her. He felt the staff at the school were discriminating against him because he was foreign. He felt very sensitive about this issue because of the racial persecution he and his family had previously experienced. He felt he had been unjustly punished by the school for his actions.

Given his past experiences, his behaviour at the school made more sense. We arranged a meeting with school staff to allow Mr Smith to tell his story in more detail. Following this, the school helped to bring parents together to discuss bullying in the school. The powerful connection made between bullying and racial persecution strengthened the school community's commitment to working on the issue more robustly. Mr Smith apologised to the parents of the children he approached. It was clear some of them were deeply moved by hearing Mr Smith's explanation for his overreaction and apologised for their children's behaviour towards his daughter.

This example illustrates working with multiple systems – the child, the family, the school. The original traumatic experience of war and persecution had increased the family's sensitivity. Helping the wider system, in this case the school, understand the traumatic past that triggered Mr Smith's behaviour allowed new commitment and enthusiasm to arise in the school's pastoral care programme. Enlisting others in the healing task facilitates conversations about traumatic experiences, reducing their powerful impact by moving them into the conversational realm – the journey from disclosure to discourse. The experience becomes reparative rather than repetitive.

When including wider kinship networks, friends and community the potential for healing to take place increases. The multiple perspectives can dilute some of the intense feelings that arise.

Opening the therapeutic space to include significant members of someone's network, either literally or metaphorically, is a cornerstone of systemic practice.

Clinicians can use the multiple aspects of self gained through membership to many systems simultaneously. Group work programmes often emphasise a particular aspect of identity. Systemic thinking can inform both the content of the group work programme and the way in which it is delivered (Rivett and Rees, 2004; Burck *et al.*, 1996). Using the group work experience to strengthen connections across generations as in CAMH Nans – a group for grandparents who care for their grandchildren and use the CAMH LAC Service; and between generations as in Dads and Lads – a group which brings together boys in the care system with men, often foster fathers; underlines the importance of *relationship* in the healing process.

Encouraging group participants to share their experiences with each other and with those at home maximises the impact of an intervention. For example, the 'self-soothing programme for living with everyday and extraordinary stress' (Smith and Lewis, unpublished) has a homework component for each group member to try the relaxation technique they have learned in the group with another family member. In the post-course follow up interviews with families, children are asked to demonstrate a technique their carer learned on the course. This is framed as an assessment of the homework component of the programme. It produces clear anecdotal evidence of transfer from the group context to the family context as the children enthusiastically demonstrate the techniques.

In working with traumatic narratives, it is essential to find the right distance for parents/primary caregivers/significant others in the work. This means they should be close enough to remain helpful but not so close as to be intrusive or traumatised themselves.

Amy, 12, is living with a foster parent. She asked to be seen as she had more 'things' she wanted to talk about but she didn't want to be seen at the hospital. When her reluctance to attend the CAMH clinic based in the hospital was explored, Amy said she was worried her mother might be listening to what she was saying. This seemed odd as she was no longer living with her mother. However, this fear related to the time when she was interviewed in the investigative suite about her injuries. Her mother had been behind the one-way screen and heard what Amy had said. In this case Amy's mother's presence was unhelpful and had inhibited Amy's disclosures. Finding a different context for her to talk was necessary.

Holding all of these competing contexts in mind is challenging. It is also easy for one to become dominant and inhibit the functioning of others. Consideration needs to given to who to invite or include in treatment sessions. Strong denial of an event perceived as traumatic by one individual can have serious consequences for the individual who seeks acknowledgement of their lived experience.

In Clinical vignette 6.1, with David's parents, it would have been unhelpful and potentially hurtful for him to have been present. Working with sub-systems towards larger gatherings can ensure more positive and constructive outcomes. For David, work with his parents ran alongside work with David and his foster mother. Before all meeting together, the adults met to talk. This included David's parents, his social worker and his foster mother. David came to his session with his parents prepared. This included having written questions he wanted to ask of his parents. He wanted his foster mother to be there as well.

Wider systems involvement

Everyone is likely to have a different perception of events, especially around traumatic events and experiences. This mismatch can also occur at wider social levels where, for example, criminal justice intervenes – a lived non-consensual experience can be reconstrued as consensual or considered false. Explaining these nuances to individuals is difficult. However, it draws attention to the multiple contexts where one can be 'confronted with accounts that radically distort the facts, including [your] own physical, emotional, mental and spiritual responses. ... [you] may have little choice but to use that language if [you] want to be treated as credible and provided with the necessary institutional support' (Wade, 2007, p. 67). It is important for therapy not to become overly organised by other discourses and at times to shed light on them.

Elaine looked after her grandchildren because her son was in prison convicted of neglect and a sexual offence against one of his children. Elaine's understanding was that her son had *raped* her grandchild. She told me he was clear that he had not done this. There was a strong belief that he had been wrongly convicted. I agreed to do some inquiring on Elaine's behalf. The court papers made clear that Elaine's son had been convicted of neglect which he pleaded guilty to and indecent assault. This had involved the child giving evidence in court. I met with Elaine and discussed what I had found out which included his conviction for indecent assault. I explained what 'indecent assault' meant from a legal point of view.

We also discussed the neglect charge. She confirmed that the children had all been neglected and that she had repeatedly gone to the house and taken the children away to wash and feed them. She thought it was unfair that only her son was convicted and wondered why his partner (mother of the children) was not also convicted. This is intertwined with the story of her son's unfair conviction.

She came back to the issue of rape – 'So he has never been convicted of rape?' – I was curious why this was so important to her. Her granddaughter was getting married and had invited her grandmother to be there after a long period of estrangement. In reconnecting with her grandmother, she had told her that she had never been raped by her dad. This activated Elaine's belief that he had been wrongly convicted. Her granddaughter said she couldn't remember what he had done to her. However, when I explained the difference between the UK legal definitions of 'rape' and 'indecent assault' Elaine confirmed that her granddaughter had disclosed the 'indecent assault' to her when she was a little girl. Elaine had believed her. In Elaine's mind this (indecent assault) was not considered as 'bad' as rape.

The use of language and local meanings had become a block to understanding between Elaine and her granddaughter. In working through this it became clear that the granddaughter was telling the truth when she said he had not raped her; he was telling the truth that he had not raped her and Elaine felt vindicated in believing her son *and* her granddaughter. The issue of his partner's failure to be prosecuted (especially in light of similar future parenting failures) remained an injustice.

Knowing how to negotiate this terrain of meanings without injury or causing offence is challenging. Sometimes it can lead to serious and longstanding family ruptures or feuds.

Community strategies

It is necessary to be aware that in some places and some families, members are inducted into an environment where 'wrong' is the norm. This was the case for Elaine's daughter-in-law, whose own life story was filled with parental failures and abuses. Trying to challenge this dominant narrative is very difficult. Many of the parents try hard not to recreate the poor parenting they experienced through parental neglect, alcohol and drug abuse, domestic violence and mental health problems. This is a triumph of creative imagination.

When traumatic experience occurs at a community level extreme behaviours provoke extreme reactions. A politician discussing the issue of how the genocide in Rwanda has affected the people suggests '... they are now indoctrinated in the ideology of genocide' (Gourevitch, 2009). Political discourses can become absorbed; incubating until a context emerges that allows an ideology to be enacted. If thought precedes the action, this state of mind is extremely dangerous. Traumatic ruminations uninterrupted can become addictive and potentially explosive.

We need to recognise the phenomena of collective trauma. Years of exposure to violence and brutality is likely to induce patterns of thinking that are 'restrictive, petty, mundane, rigid, fixed on survival and self interest' (Somasundaram, 2007).

The CAMH Nans talk about how hard it is to bring children up in communities where violence, alcohol and drugs are all around them. As Krishnamurti says (quoted in Patel, 2007, p. 235) 'It is no measure of health to be well adjusted to a profoundly sick society'. Daya Somasundaram (2007) outlines the devastating consequences following on from collective trauma after years of war in Sri Lanka. This chronic exposure results in 'the destruction of social capital, the nodal points of vibrant relationships and essential networks'.

Clinicians need to contribute to 'collaborative communities', especially in times of harsh strictures or what seem to be overwhelming constraints. This builds social capital by putting lived experience in close and harmonious relation to knowledge, skills, expertise and ethical practice.

In inviting participants to co-run programmes and increasingly moving toward group interventions, 'the experience of making a contribution to the lives of others can be a catalyst to reduce the effects (or transform the nature) of the suffering in the person's [own] life' (Denborough, 2008, p. 3). This move towards ensuring suffering is meaningful is a recurring theme in stories of resilience, recovery and reclamation.

Working together to create safer communities and considering what place therapy will occupy reflects the current move into models of public mental health focusing more on emotional wellbeing. Wide-ranging community projects often emerge as a response to collective traumatic experiences. The time makes it necessary to seek widely and move out of constraining models as healthcare moves into a contracting phase.

bell hooks (1994, quoted in Burnham and Harris, 2002, p. 29) notes that 'focusing on community rather than safety creates a sense of shared commitment and a common good that binds us all'. We need to 're-establish community processes, traditional practices, rituals, resources and relationships. ... When methods are culturally familiar, they tap into past childhood, community and religious roots and thus release a rich source of associations that can be helpful in the healing process' (Somasundaram, 2007).

Margie and Bernadette from the CAMH Nans programme, discussing their lives, noted the importance of ritual on the one hand – 'The ritual gets you through the hard times' – and the day-to-day grind – 'you just plod on' – on the other. They also shared how ritual made it possible to manage life-cycle transitions. This process of connection and reflection is captured as they reflect on the death of their mothers in Clinical vignette 6.2.

Spiritual practice

Spiritual practice is strongly associated with resilience. 'What kept our

	CLINICAL VIGNETTE 6.2	
Speaker	Spoken conversation	Clinical reflection
Margie	I can remember the first day I laughed after my mum died ... I thought my mum would look down and say to me 'Well it's about time, girl!'	The power of humour comes across and the sense of connection even after death, reflected in the conversational voice of her mother speaking to her.
Clinician	What about you Bernadette? How do you remember your mother?	
Bernadette	I feel my mum is here with me. I have ways of remembering her. Anytime I see a rainbow I think of her. I wear her ring and feel she is with me.	This shows how connections can be kept alive by the every day experiences and totems of connection.
Clinician	Do you think your grandchildren have such memories of their mothers?	This question connects the generations. It led on to the differences between generations and the management of life-cycle issues in families, in particular death.

fabric strong was spirituality, the invisible thread that binds us all' (The National Strategic Framework for Aboriginal and Torres Strait Islander Health). Bringing such a delicate theme into discussions about traumatic experience is a powerful intervention. In seeking deeper meaning and understanding for lived experiences, accessing the discourse of spiritual practice can provide comfort and distance from personal suffering. It may help to use a specific tool like the spiritual genogram (Frame, 2000).

Froma Walsh (2008) provides suggestions to help systemic clinicians feel more confident and comfortable introducing spirituality into their clinical practice. She encourages questions about religious affiliation, as well as interest about spiritual beliefs.

Having interviewed many survivors of religious abuse, it was apparent that many no longer participated in organised religion but still maintained a deep personal spiritual practice.

The Oyneg Shabes archive was dedicated to chronicling daily life in the Warsaw Ghetto during the Second World War. It consisted of a collection of daily mementos, writings and memorabilia from the Warsaw ghetto based on a feeling that 'understanding and memory had to focus not only on the collective catastrophe but also on the individual lives' (Kassow, 2007, p. 4). This reflects the interplay and importance of individual lived experience and wider collective experience. Coherence can be created by managing the multiple levels of context that operate, sometimes mysteriously, in life through relationships and conversations with others. The Oyneg Shabes archive was left to be found. It was created for an 'other' to share. It remains a testament to people's need to perform, witness and share their inner life despite overwhelming stress.

Collective narratives

David Denborough (2008) suggested a number of themes to shape collective narrative practice. These are: attention to the wider social and political issues regarding personal experience; recognising the survival aspects of experience as active rather than passive; encouraging and developing the narratives of resilience, resistance and reparation; and reinforcing intergenerational connectedness. Without this, tragedies of the individual kind can go unnoticed.

Tiffany Wright died aged three, of neglect, in a room above a pub in Sheffield on 28 September 2007. 'Her case challenges the British notion of community ... family and friends, neighbours, pub regulars, staff all watched as a sickening child faded from view and not one of them called for help' (Levy and Scott-Clark, 2010).

This child death is not a single incident. Pressures of work, fear of bankruptcy and relationship difficulties all contributed to the neglect of this child – these worries filled the mind of her primary caregivers and Tiffany was no longer in anyone's mind until she was found dead.

Acknowledgement of traumatic experience is part of the recovery process (Tomm, 2002; Tomm and Govier, 2007). Acknowledgement in a wider context, such as family or community, creates a shared reality. It allows for recognition not only of the trauma but also of all the small acts of resistance and kindness that are embedded as the often 'not yet said' aspect of the story.

Public and private ritual

Rituals and reparation serve an important function in acknowledging traumatic experience but ultimately they don't make it go away or change the fact that it happened.

In Clinical vignette 6.3 Margie shares her family's journey to understanding and recovery from the traumatic death of her eldest brother while he was evacuated during the Second World War.

CLINICAL VIGNETTE 6.3	
Spoken conversation	**Clinical reflection**
Georgie slipped on the threshing machine ... He was my mum's favourite.	The significance of this interjection about being mum's favourite comes out as the story unfolds.
I remember his body coming home. It was in our parlour.	This is part of the traumatic memory – the body coming home – but the ritual of laying the body out in the parlour is a community practice to help with grief and mourning.
He was 14. Me mum blamed the farmers ... she said it was their fault	This has been the family story for many years. Opening discussions regarding blame is extremely important. Often people have strongly held ideas about whom or what is to blame for bad things that happen.
We were all traumatised by it ... me mum cried for two years ... My mother never dealt with that trauma.	This reflection demonstrates the wide impact of a traumatic experience on the whole family.
We (his siblings) had to deal with it. My brother who was with him on the farm didn't know his brother was dead until he came home. Nobody told him.	The siblings didn't deal with it until significantly many years after their mother's death.
When he slipped, the threshing machine severed his foot and he was taken to hospital. The hospital recommended the leg	This is the story of Georgie's death. Despite finding the fare and waiting for train tracks to clear after bombings the parents arrived too late

CLINICAL VIGNETTE 6.3 *Continued*	
Spoken conversation	**Clinical reflection**
was amputated but the farmer wouldn't agree. He said it was too big a decision for him to make. They sent for my parents in Liverpool. They had to find the fare because they had no money. The train was stopped in Crewe because of the bombing so they couldn't get through and by the time they reached the hospital gangrene had set in.	to save their son. When Margie shared this part of the story there was a long silence in the group.
We went back to the farm. The story of our Georgie had been passed on to their grand-children. They were traumatised by it as well. ˙	This occurs many years later. That the story of Georgie's death is being passed down through his host family meant a lot to Margie and her siblings. It was the beginning of hearing a different account and recognition that the host family shared their trauma.
The story was completely different to the one my mum told. The farmers had hired the machine and kept it in a shed. Georgie was chasing a rat and slipped. My mum always said he had been working on the machine. The farmer's wife wrapped his foot, held him, went with him to hospital and had me mum's hate for all of her life.	The competing narrative unfolds. Margie was asked to reflect on her mother's feelings towards the farmer's wife and to consider her mother's shame at not being able to hold Georgie when he was injured and how her plan to protect him by sending him to the country during the war had failed.
We found out our Georgie had a girl … You know they weren't going to come back to Liverpool. Our Ronnie said 'You know Margie we loved it there we weren't going to come home. I didn't tell mum because I felt guilty'.	The idea that Georgie had life plans that didn't involve him returning home brought him 'alive' and facilitated his brother speaking for the first time to his sisters about what had happened all those years ago.

Our interdependence can be a resource. Together we can foster resilience as it is a 'product of close collaboration and mutual co-construction between individual and collective' (Papadopoulos and Hildebrand, 1997). Margie's journey was done with a sister and shared with her other siblings.

> After we did our journey, my brother spoke about it for the first time – he said he couldn't speak because he didn't want to upset mum. He lived all of his adult life saying it should have been me not our Georgie.

This is classic survivor guilt. The family story of Georgie as the favoured son will have increased Ronnie's feelings that he was more expendable than his brother.

Families often bring children to treatment to be 'fixed' without appreciating how they can be involved, perhaps crucially to the 'fixing'.

> My mum got stuck. She could have received so much comfort by sharing with the farmer's family. They loved him too. We planted a rose and put up a plaque in the barn. Think of the comfort she would have had from that ...

Contributing to the healing process touches on the wider context of community, that has benefits all round. This experience prompted Margie to seek out wider connections and consider the social and political issues involved with the evacuee programmes.

> We joined the evacuee organisation and asked our MP to find out how many children died when they were evacuated. They did a plaque and put all their names in a book – our Georgie was there in gold ... it was recognition that our Georgie's life hadn't been wasted.

Contributing to supporting others through their traumatic experiences led the CAMH Nans and Grandads to donate handkerchiefs 'for those times when tissues aren't enough'. The following is written on the home made boxes.

> Cotton, linen, flowered, plain ... please choose one out of our special box which is filled with love and hope ... These handkerchiefs represent someone is listening, cares ... reminds us we are not alone but one of many ...

They have often become a talking point in therapy; from bemused wonder about what they are and how to use them to positive memories about 'hankies' and grandparents. Though many are taken away, new ones always arrive or old ones return washed and pressed. This simple act, the provision of cotton handkerchiefs, has come to signify a number of things:

1. It is okay to cry.
2. Men cry too (we have man-size hankies).
3. Hankies hold more tears.
4. Other people come here and cry too.

In a way they represent the 'felt' experience. While talk is good, felt is better.

There can be times when talking is not helpful or beneficial. 'Co-rumination', which dwells on problems and self blame, can make individuals feel worse, especially teenage girls (Rose, 2002; Rose et al., 2007). This connects with problem-saturated narratives. This needs to be kept in mind when running group work programmes or family sessions as they can easily become dominated by traumatic stories which are overwhelming for everyone – the speaker, the listeners and the facilitators. Finding the right balance between acknowledging trauma and simultaneously highlighting acts of resilience and resistance is key.

Being in a group encourages shared experience and reduces isolation. The group becomes a community intent on emotional wellbeing. It emphasises interconnectedness.

The importance of opening up therapeutic discourse to wider cultural influences is vital – life giving. A fear of death or dying often removes that vitality. In Clinical vignette 6.4 Margie and Bernadette from the CAMH Nans are discussing death.

CLINICAL VIGNETTE 6.4		
Speaker	**Spoken conversation**	**Clinical reflection**
Margie	In those days they brought the coffin home. It made death a part of our life.	This touches on changes over time and different generational experiences of life-cycle events.

Speaker	Spoken conversation	Clinical reflection
Bernadette	Having them home before they were buried was important. It became your final time with them.	This is a shared cultural experience for both women despite a ten year age gap. There is also the ritual of closure and goodbyes.
Margie	Death has no fear for me – it was a place where you finished.	As death was so much part of her growing up experience, it becomes another life-cycle event.
Clinician	Is it important to have rituals?	
Bernadette	Ritual helps you deal with it ... it marks an end.	The theme of endings and closure returns.
Margie	It was part of community ... I remember as children we used to go and ask if we could see Mrs. Such n Such ... (laughing).	This reinforces the community aspect of death as a life-cycle transition. It also shows the child's curiosity. Later in the group there was discussion about how some children found the practice very disturbing.
Bernadette	There's not many that come home now.	Reflecting changes in practice – what takes its place?
Margie	No I don't know of any but we have to talk about it ... it's the cycle of life as you get older maybe it is easier ... I'm on my last cycle now (said humorously).	Talking about death becomes a substitute and there is a generational reflection. The strong sense of humour comes across in Margie joking about her own life cycle stage.
Clinician	You're not coming back then Margie?	
Margie	No ... I'm staying up there if it's okay ... if it's not I'll have to protest and come back down again.	Protest has kept Margie going for years.

The use of ritual, humour and the power of protest are clearly in evidence. These are all aspects of resilience. Enabling cross generational conversations to take place opens dialogues about change.

'Ritual is not only an act of collective memory; it is art continually refinished; and it is value reconfirmed ... Under girding all ritual is the faith and assurance that it will survive' (Rosenblatt, 2000). Of course change is inevitable and protest is often a way to promote changes. This paradox of wanting to keep rituals which reinforce the status quo and represent stability is juxtaposed with protest, the desire to change things for the better.

Creative acts become a form of resistance. Taking away a people's language is often one of the first steps in oppressive regimes, which is why the articulated disclosure needs to unfold into discursive narrative. When spoken words are not available, or perhaps not enough, other art forms exist. The act of creating brings people together – language can sometimes be a barrier that music, visual arts or dance transcend. They can all be interwoven with narrative practices.

For example, the Dandelion Trust uses the traditional group singing of Georgia to 'create harmony and resolve trauma'. Singing involves stories set to music. Madge Bray (Bray and Kane, 2006) describes the powerful messages contained within the lyrics and the shared experiences of singing them out loud.

Rats mtrobas daungrevia, siqvaruls ushenebia.
(What hatred has destroyed, love can rebuild.)

Bateson went so far as to say: 'Mere purposive rationality unaided by such phenomena as art, religion, dream and the like is necessarily pathogenic and destructive of life' (Bateson, 1973, p. 119; Flemons, 1991, p. 93). This encourages clinicians to incorporate more creativity into systemic work.

Apologies and acts of reparation

An apology or an act of reparation needs careful consideration. Who is it being done for? Sometimes it is to make the apologist feel better. For victims, the intention can sometimes not be discerned clearly or the genuineness of the apology remains in doubt. Feelings change over time – an apology once accepted can later feel unaccepted.

Balancing the collective need for restitution and reparation against individual needs for healing and peace of mind brings two very different levels of systems together, not always successfully.

Moving towards positions of forgiveness is made more difficult 'in [the] inability at times to reconcile the past as really past, thus leaving [the] present open to an ongoing haunting by the past'(Ricoeur, 1999, p. 164). Reconciling the past means letting it go and in doing so some aspect of identity will be lost forever. Individuals may not be confident enough in their capacity to create new identities or find new meanings in life. Relinquishing the past could also feel like betrayal.

This is a fundamentally important issue. If traumatic experience remains unprocessed, then there may be periods of time when it seems the past is gone but then suddenly and unexpectedly the past becomes present.

Margaret in thinking about her son, who killed himself after committing a serious violent crime, couldn't bury him. It was as if all that was good about him seemed to vanish and he didn't deserve a burial, a place to be remembered. It felt inappropriate to mourn him. Every year, on his birthday and the anniversary of his death, she was reminded that she still had not found a resting place for him. This connected to her story of herself as a bad mother. She felt responsible for his criminal activities and his suicide. When she was able to reclaim her identity as a good mother, she was able to bury her son.

Time acted as a reminder for Margaret. Time also acted as a reminder for Donna. She had had a late termination which was very traumatic. She felt very guilty and ashamed about this. She became very depressed.

Donna was given a ritual to help her move on from the guilt she felt regarding her termination. She was encouraged to talk of her baby. This was something she had not allowed herself to do. She provided the baby with a name and set aside a time each year to remember the baby. The local church had a small chapel for children where parents could leave mementos to commemorate and mark their child's life. By keeping the baby in mind, rather than the act for which she felt shame, she began to feel less depressed. This allowed her to review why she made the decision she did and how she was unsupported by those most important to her when she went through this ordeal.

The baby represented a story once untellable and unheard that through the narrative process became healing. New stories should move 'from blame and labelling to positive connotation and contextualisation, from linearity to circularity' (Selekman, 1997, p. 14). They should be future-oriented, dreaming, imagining and appreciative (Lang and McAdam, 1997). They usually feature directional shifts in time, space, causality, interactions, values and telling (Sluzki, 1992). They are full of reflexive wonder (Cronen and Pearce 1980; Cronen 2001).

Conclusion

This capacity to take the best and honour it is the hallmark of resilience. Forgiveness and reconciliation opens up the territory of the heart – the felt experience and creative force of life. Opening up this territory, through relationships and interconnectedness, requires involvement of family, friends and community in the therapeutic process. Otherwise, therapy may become the only place the client feels alive – a strange inversion.

The felt experience of a good therapeutic encounter needs to ripple out into wider relational networks to be sustained over time. This potentially allows the resilience and resistance to develop and become the dominant story. The wider acknowledgement of trauma paradoxically allows it to be remembered as past. 'You are not just surviving – You are alive' (Rober in Wilson, 2007).

Helping families come to terms with traumatic experience is like panning for gold – trying to find something essential and positive to remember and honour.

7

SUPERVISION IN TRAUMA WORK

Introduction

This chapter explores systemic supervision with specific reference to trauma work and life-cycle issues. It includes a discussion of vicarious traumatisation and some of the symptoms associated with it. The focus is on supervision as a practice of reflection and strengthening personal competence (Bertrando, 2007) rather than for didactic purposes (Fruggeri, 2002). Our capacity to be self reflective is essential when considering the complexities and emotionally charged issues presented in trauma work. The importance of developing a programme of self-care to maintain clinical boundaries and integrity of clinical practice is essential.

Role of supervision

Supervision needs to be more than finding the 'right way' to do something. In this respect Cecchin's notion of irreverence as a way of giving voice to doubt and uncertainty should be encouraged in the supervision context (Cecchin *et al.*, 1994). Supervision can help clinicians remain 'receptive' to new material (Andersen, 1987) and reflective on what is produced within a session (Burck and Campbell, 2002; Burnham, 1993; Rober, 2005). Anyone engaged in mental-health work will be exposed to many traumatic lived experiences, mostly past but some also present, with the spectre of repeated traumatic experience looming in the future. This can also include personal traumatic experiences, not solely those of clients.

Within supervision, clinicians tend not to bring transcripts or recordings but an account of the session. The details and feelings have already been filtered. Reflecting on excluded material or remembering uncomfortable feelings is likely to open up new conversations – the not yet said (Anderson and Goolishian, 1992).

Clearly, live supervision allows a different kind of synergistic experience to emerge. Lowenstein, Reder and Clark (1982) describe the 'intense emotions provoked by live supervision such as anxiety, shame, fear of exposure, loss of autonomy, [and potential] challenges to competence'. In trauma work, it is likely that the affective component of the work for client and clinician will be tricky to deal with, ranging from avoidance to highly volatile. Lee and Littlejohns (2006) also draw attention to the 'self doubt and anxiety' supervision of clinical work can raise.

Bringing vulnerabilities to supervision requires a good relationship with the supervisor, clear boundaries, time and space to consider difficult emotional issues without moving into the realms of personal therapy.

This touches on the different positions a supervisor might occupy simultaneously (manager and supervisor) and perhaps explains what material is then brought to the supervision context. Supervision within a busy working environment can easily become a tick box exercise or quick case review. Once qualified, the teaching aspect of continuing professional development is much more subordinated: reflection on practice predominates.

Live supervision adds more complexity through the mutually influencing systems of family, clinician, supervision group and supervisor. Reflecting on the positions taken during sessions and within supervision contexts can be helpful. A fixed point of view inhibits the creation of alternative stories. Traumatic material is especially prone to becoming fixed and in turn constraining of new stories emerging.

Supervision is a 'metalogue'. This is defined by Bateson (quoted in Flemons, 1991, p. 3) as a type of dialogue where 'not only do the participants discuss [a] problem but the structure of the conversation as a whole is also relevant to the same subject'. Andersen (1987) referred to supervision as a meta-dialogue – a dialogue about a dialogue.

It is an ethical duty and therapeutic responsibility to reflect on personal prejudices when working with systems (Cecchin, 1987, p. 409). Fredman (2004) encourages consideration to be given to 'response-ability' in clinical work. This touches on the dual process of listening and acting on what has been introduced into the conversation. This is a reminder of the importance that 'language [is] a form of action rather than just a form of representation'. Supervision is an essential part of professional development and fosters the process of acting and reflecting on the shared stories emerging from clinical work.

Clinicians need to work towards making their practice 'relevant, desired, meaningful and accountable' (Denborough, 2006, p. 47).

Trauma-specific supervision issues

Trauma work requires clear boundaries to be maintained so that clinicians and clients are not traumatised or re-traumatised by the therapeutic exchange. Feelings and reactions need to be processed outside of the client–clinician relationship safely and appropriately (Mosley and Wiewel, 2011). Boundary violations within therapy are harmful. Supervision is a forum to remind clinicians of this.

Traumatic material can block this receptivity by activating emotional deregulation in the clinician through overloading with overwhelming negative emotional material (Mosley and Wiewel, 2011). This 'client–clinician emotional disregulation' can become stuck on hypersensitivity, characterised by increasing anxiety or dissociative emotionally cut-off interactions within therapy sessions (Mosley and Wiewel, 2011).

Clinical supervision is discussed and investigated less often than other aspects of clinical practice (Kilminster and Jolly, 2000). Research suggests that less experienced clinicians tend to be more vulnerable to secondary traumatisation (McLean and Wade, 2003). A survey undertaken in 2008 by Unison, the public sector union, reported a quarter of its participants felt practice supervision had deteriorated in the last five years. Community Care, a social work publication, highlighted in a research review that 28 per cent of participants reported not receiving any supervision at all and a further 31 per cent felt supervision to be inadequate for their caseload (Hunter, 2009). The professionals surveyed are not systemic practitioners, but this reflects organisational constraints placed on practice supervision for professionals involved in demanding and stressful social care work, despite repeated public inquiries underlining its importance.

Good supervision should help clinicians consider 'exposing the selves behind the professional masks' (Traynor, 1998). We also need to consider that in general 'we do not like accounts that render us powerless' (Groen and Van Lawick, 2009, p. 232). More specifically Martine Groen writes of the failure to discuss 'it' [by this I am taking her to mean trauma] as a manifestation of 'the therapist taking on the client's shame'. Together dignity is preserved by not discussing 'it'.

Stories of victimhood are considered more acceptable than stories of perpetration. Consider for example individuals who are traumatised by their own actions (McNally, 2010). This has been documented in the case of war veterans (Lifton, 1973 quoted in McNally, 2010) and embedded in the concept of 'self traumatised perpetrator' (Young, 2002). McNally writes 'conventional moral categories would classify these veterans as perpetrators of trauma not victims of trauma. ... our current concept of trauma does not address the self traumatised perpetrator' [enough] (McNally, 2010, p. 389).

Supervision for those who work with perpetrators needs to take into consideration this collective avoidance. Holding on to issues of responsibility in client groups who are likely to distort, minimise and deny the offensive acts they have perpetrated may need a more structured supervision approach like the caucuses used by the Just Therapy group (Waldegrave and Tamasese, 1993). This ensures the experience and voice of the 'victim' or marginalised group is kept in focus in therapeutic work aimed at changing patterns of traumatic offending.

Vicarious traumatisation

In working systemically with trauma, consideration needs to be given to the potentially isomorphic process of vicarious traumatisation (Liddle, 1988; Liddle and Saba, 1983; White and Russell, 1997). Judith Herman went so far as to say 'If a therapist finds herself isolated in her professional practice, she should discontinue working with traumatised patients until she has secured an adequate support system' (Herman, 1997, p. 153). Chronic exposure to disturbing events can challenge fundamental beliefs about the safety and security of the world. While research on supervision is scarce, there is even less on how we feel about our work.

However, emotional responses such as depression, mild anxiety, emotional exhaustion and disrupted relationships are reported for mental health professionals (Brady, Healy et al. 1995, cited in Norcross, 2000). Clinicians can experience professional isolation increased by 'the imperatives of confidentiality' and feel unable to discuss 'not coping' with the work (Baruch, 2004; Figley, 1995; Gilroy et al., 2002; Norcross and Guy, 2007).

There is the strange paradox that bringing doubt and uncertainty, personal vulnerabilities and confusions into the work context can seem to undermine professionalism. Systemically this complex interplay of personal and professional experience needs continual attention as clinicians move in and out of performing identities. Supervision needs to make a safe enough context for this to happen.

As a basic premise, supervision is seen as an essential part of professional practice. There is an ethical duty to ensure that supervision takes place (Storm *et al.*, 2001). Within trauma work, the potential for secondary traumatisation is much greater given the exposure to the toxic emotional experiences of others (Figley, 1995; Jenmorri, 2006; Pearlman and Saakvitne, 1995). The sensitivity that contributes to being a good clinician increases the risk for secondary traumatisation. Specific characteristics that contribute to being a good clinician, such as being warm, open or empathically connected, also predispose an individual to vicarious traumatisation.

If this is not dealt with, vicarious traumatisation can manifest in working practices through high levels of absenteeism, for example, but perhaps more subtly in the dominant narratives that become privileged in the clinical context. Cases become 'hopeless'. 'Burnout' can result when the balance between what is given and what is received becomes overly skewed towards giving (Hawkins and Shohet, 2007, p. 222). In extreme forms this can be described as 'helperholism' – an addiction to help others. The Foresight Project on Mental Capital and Wellbeing (2008) raised the issue of 'presenteeism' at work where workers are physically present but not productively working. Their report suggests this could cost the UK £900 million a year.

In reflecting on 'professional burnout', the literature describes the gradual erosion of self care in the work place – tardiness, failure to complete tasks, taking on more work or not working at all.

Using Roland Summit's categories (Summit, 1983) Tony Morrison (1990, 2005) described how child protection workers often go through identifiable phases of: helplessness; secrecy; entrapment and accommodation; delayed and unconvincing disclosure; retraction. Safeguarding work involves exposure to traumatic material.

In considering what helps reduce stress in the workplace (Himle *et al.*, 1989) the role of supervision was considered pivotal. This has also been raised in countless public inquiries.

Without access to good clinical supervision professionals can become subject to dominant narratives of hopelessness, failure and blame. This can promote 'presenteeism' – *doing* at work without *being* at work – the physical presence but soulful absence of the workforce. This disruption to beliefs of basic safety and security can lead to professional burnout and avoidance of doing work that reinforces this destabilised view. Life experiences, especially distressing and traumatic ones, interact with professional identities. Supervision can raise the question: 'How does trauma therapy stretch us as practitioners and how do we choose to respond to this call?' (Jenmorri, 2006, p. 50).

Consideration needs to be given to the emotional and physical impact of clinical trauma work. The emotional centre of the brain is operating far in advance of the more cerebral integrating and analysing centres. High levels of expressed emotion can activate the fight or flight responses. The 'physiological effects of anxiety', (Lee and Littlejohns, 2006, p. 242) can paralyse creative thinking and practice.

Intrusive flashbacks not from your experience

Clinicians need space to discuss aversive reactions to the material presented in trauma work. This needs to include discussion of the lasting images or fragments of disturbing case material that remain when sessions have finished.

It is important to specifically track intrusive thoughts or images from cases that are coming up out of context. It is more difficult to track avoidance issues as this is the material least likely to be brought to supervision.

Clinicians need to be 'close enough but safe enough' to follow the story and consider its implications. While 'reflection on action' is an important part of supervision, 'reflection in action' (Schön, 1987) is of equal importance. This is where the midbrain responses activated by high-expressed negative emotions such as fear can override our analytical capacities. This can happen within a session.

Shame and other 'unacceptable' feelings

Clinical work can touch highly emotional personal issues and traumatic experiences. A clinician may feel shameful about this and unable to share it in supervision. Shame can block access to emotional information. So 'shameful' moments in clinical work may be the least likely to be discussed in supervision (Kavner and McNab, 2005). A 'dialogical self functions as a "society of mind" with tensions, conflicts and contradictions as intrinsic features of a (healthy functioning) self' (Bertrando, 2007, p. 150; Hermans and Dimaggio, 2007). This complexity needs to include those shameful moments. Traumatic process stops 'reflection in action'. Supervision can help facilitate 'reflection on action' (Schön, 1987, p. 47). This complexity needs to include those shameful moments. There are other feelings that seem less acceptable to discuss.

The therapeutic literature is biased towards promoting forgiveness (James, 2007, p. 136). This theme can constrain supervision conversations – sometimes being able to talk about the anger, outrage and/or disgust felt is essential. A supervision context needs to allow time for consideration, reflection and processing these feelings prior to raising highly emotive issues with families.

In telling their stories, clients may also not share aspects of self they feel shame about. Additionally, aspects where undesired behaviours are shared – for example hitting in a family where domestic violence has been an issue – can be difficult to discuss. It is often easier to locate the entire problem in one person – the family scapegoat. The scapegoat of course was sent out into the wilderness, presumably to die or at least never return.

Consider Clinical vignette 7.1. The family has been referred following domestic violence. An eight-year-old boy, Darren, is attending with his mother and his 14-year-old sister.

CLINICAL VIGNETTE 7.1

Speaker	Spoken conversation	Clinical reflection
Clinician	So do you argue with your sister sometimes?	This question moves into the 'territory' of arguments. It can be used to explore the issue of safe and unsafe arguments.
Darren	Yes ... not sometimes *all the time.*	'All the time' signals to the clinician an imbalance – too much arguing.
Clinician	So what happens in these arguments with your sister?	Curiosity is used to open the discussion.
Darren	I just hit her.	This blunt matter of fact response shocks the clinician.
Clinician	Pardon [incredulity].	The clinician is questioning whether they have heard what the boy said correctly.
Darren	I just hit her.	Same matter of fact tone suggests this type of behaviour is seen as 'normal'. *Continued*

CLINICAL VIGNETTE 7.1 *Continued*		
Speaker	**Spoken conversation**	**Clinical reflection**
Clinician	Do you hit her first; is that what the arguments are about, you hitting her?	The invitation to see it as normal brings about a parental response from the clinician.
Darren	No when I stand by her she just pushes me so I hit her back ... she grabs me like that (indicates hands clasped around his chin with force) ... and it hurts.	The detailed description is bordering on an enactment. The argument seems to be about space and standing your ground. The age gap between the siblings is six years. There is a clash of generation and gender – eight-year-old boy and 14-year-old girl.
Mother	Yes but it's not been her who starts them all of the time ... you go in the room sometimes and just jump on her and smack her or if you can't have your way throw something at her ...	When Mother intervenes it is to support her daughter.

This brief interaction highlights how violence has come to live in this family – it is a regular visitor. It is shocking in its intensity and takes the clinician by surprise. Many families do not want to talk about *it* and see the removal of the perpetrator (often the father figure) as *the solution*. This avoidance can be seen as a result of trauma, but it needs to be addressed as the potential for traumatic enactments is extremely high. The description given by mum in the vignette seems shockingly familiar. It was difficult for the clinician to raise this obvious isomorphism at the time because he had become overly organised with the idea of the father as the sole perpetrator of violence and felt constrained as a male to challenge the mother's defence of her daughter. He also found the description of family violence disturbing.

This is an example of Bateson's idea that 'All that is not information ... is noise and that noise is the only possible source of new patterns' (Bateson, 1967 quoted in Papadopoulos, 2002, p. 160). It is clear from this brief transcript that hitting was not the exclusive domain of the father. This interchange could easily be disregarded as so called noise as it was not what the family had come to discuss.

Supervision and live supervision most directly encourages the development of 'skills to discriminate between information and data and to increase effectiveness in eliciting appropriate information' (Papadopoulos, 2002, p. 159). This attention to 'noise' is easily missed in retrospective supervision. Similarly, the felt experience of the clinician in the room can be easily overlooked.

Clinicians' beliefs about the therapeutic process

The centrality of the clinician within the therapeutic experience can affect vulnerability to vicarious traumatisation. It can feel pressurised to be in a central expert position in clinical practice. Systemic practices such as 'not knowing' and 'outsider witnessing', where significant others are invited to a clinical consultation to offer personal reflections and comments to the material (White, 2005b, p. 15), move the systemic clinician into more collaborative approaches. One clinician, reflecting on her experience of 'outsider witnessing', commented 'I am now less willing to be drawn into supplying the answers and am instead finding ways to draw out answers' (Fox et al., 2002). This less central position and diminished sense of sole responsibility for change will offer some protection for clinicians from vicarious traumatisation.

With trauma work, the clinician acts as the other or is prepared to lend themselves to the process in order to introduce difference – new information (Smith, 2005a, b). This openness increases the risk for vicarious traumatisation. Supervisors need to be mindful of this, as it may be that the clinician does not recognise the potential risk or feels constrained from raising it.

A number of other factors have been identified that make stressful work more stressful (McLean and Wade, 2003). These include not only certain beliefs about therapy but also recent personal stressors, higher caseloads and less clinical experience.

In this study the following beliefs were considered risk factors for burnout:

Clinicians feeling overly responsible for the change process;
Clinicians' avoidance of strong emotions;
Clinicians' rigid adherence to or over reliance on a model/ programme.

These core findings confirm previous studies (Bloom, 1997; Bloom and Farragher, 2011; Figley, 1995; Pearlman and Saakvitne, 1995; Rivett and Rees, 2008).

What's not in the manual

Focusing on technique and method – more easily taught and measured for success – perhaps misses some of the more subtle aspects of therapeutic work – the impact of work on the clinician's own family and personal identity. Bateson (Flemons, 1991, p. 123) referred to the more left-brained approach to therapy as 'manipulative techniques' even if 'poetically and aesthetically correct' but essentially dead. A privileging of intellectual/evidence based manual approaches to therapeutic work, rather than a phenomenological approach to clinical practice, can lead to sterile therapeutic encounters.

Manualising or programming systemic interventions may contribute to the loss of 'vitality through codification' (Gergen and Gergen, 2010, p. 258). It may be helpful to consider whether this move towards manualisation is a way of diluting or minimising vicarious traumatisation. It can suspend emotional engagement with the material clients present. This can be a protective action for the clinician but leave the client feeling unheard.

For example, in a manualised self-soothing programme, session five focuses on nurturing touch and its role in affect regulation. In Clinical vignette 7.2 one of the participants, a grandmother from the kinship care programme, tells this story triggered by the educational component of the programme.

This situation is clearly not in the manual but it is highly significant for Grandma and the strong visual element of her story – the trigger picture – is still in her head. Supervision needs to be able to make space for the unexpected. Some of the supervision issues that arose included: Is it okay to physically comfort clients when they cry? What do I do when a client is 'off' programme? Do I stick with what they discuss? How can I get them back on programme?

Pointing out that by asking what she *did* the clinician moved the discussion into stories of resistance helped the group worker 'let go of the programme' and feel more confident systemically in using the feedback from the material.

Supervision needs to review and discuss unhelpful clinician beliefs that contribute to vulnerability. This includes individual clinicians feeling responsible for change as well as concern over making 'mistakes' in therapy.

CLINICAL VIGNETTE 7.2

Speaker	Spoken conversation	Clinical reflection
Grandma	I remember one time when I went over to check on the kids – they [her son and daughter-in-law, both drug users] often wouldn't let me in – Rosie was just a baby – I insisted and there she was in her cot covered in shit – I mean literally it was all over the cot, the child, her mouth, hands [grandma starts to cry ... a group member puts their hand on her shoulder ...].	As she talks about this memory, she begins to remember her feelings at the time. This suggests it is a peak episode. The group clearly feels connected as someone comforts her. It is a nonverbal gesture that is offered as comfort – a felt experience.
Clinician	What did you do?	Choosing to focus on doing helps to dilute the emotional intensity and may give evidence of resistance and/or resilience in the face of over whelming emotion.
Grandma	I picked her up and I took her – I just pushed past them and said 'this is a disgrace' and I took the poor wee thing home to mine; washed her and fed her ... that's why I cuddle her so much now. It breaks my heart thinking of her like that ...	This response shows her strength and includes a link back to the present material being discussed in the group – the importance of touch. It also shows how a past event of extreme neglect still shapes her current behaviour – 'that's why I cuddle her so much now'.

Peer group supervision

Regular peer group supervision can also create a context where clinicians can use each other's experiences and knowledge to support clinical practice.

While working at the London rape crisis centre, in addition to our regular business meetings we also had small group peer supervision. This involved discussing any calls or issues arising from work on the phone line. This collective support was vital and formed a wide 'peer-spective' on the emotive topic of rape. It helped to process distressing aspects of calls and maintained some of the key principles of the work – a believing stance towards women who called; a belief system that maintained women were not responsible for rape; a political understanding of the wider influences that condone and encourage rape as a form of patriarchal oppression. It helped maintain a climate of openness about work and facilitated reconnection to the theoretical underpinnings of the collective practice.

Supervision can help to provide a range of different points of view. It introduces the 'other' and opens the dialogue between the view taken at the time and the other possibilities. This may include a focus on the intention of interventions and the more spiritual intuitive aspects of lived experience.

Working in teams helps to keep clinicians connected to a collective practice which will develop into 'collective narrative time lines' (Denborough, 2008, p. 144). These timelines serve as an invitation for each member 'to share powerful personal memory and history but in a way that is linked to a collective theme' (Denborough, 2008, p. 144). This allows the team to take a meta-view on individual functioning – to be the 'outsider witnesses' to clinical practice.

Teams have strengths that are missing from collections of individuals. Often, however, we expect them to function healthily without paying any serious attention to team building, or to the tension that lies between interdependence and individuality. Teams do not work by chance and neither do they get into a mess by chance. But for teams to function well issues of identity, needs and power must be tackled openly (Morrison, 1990).

There needs to be space for professional stories that underline resilience and the ability to carry on doing such emotionally charged work (Jenmorri, 2006) while keeping the possibility of change alive.

When the personal and professional collide

In working with traumatic material it is possible that avoidance will lead to omitting to discuss the very aspects of the experience that are disturbing, including those aspects of the clinician's personal life-story that may be triggered in certain situations. Monica McGoldrick (1982) developed the idea of trigger families, where the clinical material being presented resonates strongly with personal issues for the clinician. There may be 'parallel patterns of meanings and emotions' (Flaskas, 1997, p. 270) between the family and clinician. Not being open about these issues could lead to poor professional practice and/or unhelpful therapeutic experiences. Clinical supervision should enable clinicians to use personal experiences and resonances with clients as resources. Being exposed to the traumatic experiences of others can also reactivate material from personal experiences.

Chris who had suffered with depression for much of her life was discussing with her clinician her thoughts about killing herself. As Chris talked about killing herself, she said she was worried about her children finding her and how upsetting this would be for them. The clinician burst into tears. This strong affective response to the material presented in the session related to a personal issue for the clinician. In supervision the clinician was able to consider what the comment from the client had triggered and consider how they might use the experience in their clinical work. The strong emotional response was viewed as a resource. Supervision included a review of the generational positions of both the clinician and Chris. Chris was much older than the clinician. She was a parent and the clinician childless. The conversation about children finding their dead parent served as a point of traumatic connection for the two of them. Sharing this in the clinical work strengthened their therapeutic relationship. The clinician's strong emotional response provided Chris with an answer to the impact her suicide might have on her children.

Making space to discuss and support clinicians working in close proximity to powerful emotional experience needs a context which balances both the personal and professional within organisational structures that seem increasingly to emphasise corporate aims and performance management.

Supervision can help workers identify personal triggers. Reflecting on life-cycle issues can help to position or activate certain aspects of identity more prominently and helpfully.

Research suggests a significant portion of those involved in mental health work will have had adverse childhood experiences themselves (Hartman and Jackson, 1994). Finding a balance in sharing personal information needs consideration. Some clients feel personal disclosures from clinicians are unhelpful and in some cases disturbing, but others may feel it helps to have a shared personal experience. It may be best to err on the cautious side when it comes to personal disclosures, as it can be very difficult for clients to raise discomfort with a clinician's personal disclosures at the time.

A healthy working environment can make such experiences a resource rather than a hindrance.

> At the start of the year I was getting bogged down in intellectually understanding cases. I was finding myself getting what I can only describe as depressed and mashed in the head. Issues from work were bleeding into my social/romantic/bedroom life. Through peer and formal supervision, I was able to reconnect *emotionally* to my work and also to discover that the feelings I was having were understandable. I'm not the first person to have them. It led me to re-evaluate who I am in my work and what parts of myself I use.
>
> Interestingly I knew cognitively about vicarious trauma but experiencing it was a different matter completely. I always thought – oh with my background [a strong loving family] I'll be fine. Errol

This demonstrates how a secure safe world view can become destabilised by constant exposure to traumatic material. It also shows that boundaries between systems (in this case work life and personal life) are permeable – recursively interlinked.

The human discourse – why do this work and how personal experience can be used effectively and helpfully with clients – is discussed less often. This desire for personal suffering to have meaning beyond the personal is often what brings individuals into healing work in the first place.

Maintaining professional boundaries helps to create the safe space for clients to bring highly emotive personal issues. Unfortunately, some clinicians violate those boundaries through inappropriate sexual relationships, many of which will have started by disclosure of personal information by the clinician.

Burnham (1993) reminds us to avoid confusing self reflexivity with self preoccupation.

In engaging with clients who have been traumatised, clinicians can be hoping to magically inoculate themselves against similar trauma.

> I remember taking a call on the rape crisis line – at the time calls were taken at home. This literally brought traumatic material into my safe space. The call had been especially upsetting with the caller repeatedly asking and sobbing 'Why me? Why me?'. When I finished the call and my time on duty I had to drive to a social engagement. As I drove around the roundabout at Elephant and Castle (London, England) with the call still going around my head,

I was hit by another car trying to enter the roundabout – a strange isomorphism – 'Why me? Why me?'.

I cite the specific place in part because of its significance – it was my first ever car accident. Secondly, as a Canadian, roundabouts (North American translation: traffic circles) in the UK have always been challenging. It represents one of those 'moments charged with the significance of memory' (Mullan, 2007).

It goes to the heart of traumatic experience – failure to anticipate it happening contributes to its devastation and attacks the sense of self that believes in the predictability of experience.

Colleagues who have worked in contexts where safety cannot be taken for granted have to find ways 'to maintain an internalised "acceptable level of fear"' (Reilly, 1999, p. 231).

When I first started doing safeguarding work I saw abuse *everywhere* and talked about it all the time. I wonder what that has turned into? Cynicism? Resignation? Expecting less from the world?
Errol

Errol's quote captures the sometimes profound changes working with traumatic material produces in how the world is seen. It can undermine basic concepts of safety and security.

There were times ... when stories of terrible atrocities were shared with us, when I would be determined to take action ... Through conversations of accountability with the families and black workers ... I heard ... I was not being asked to take up a cause 'on behalf of'

This reflection from Vanessa Swan (1998) captures the desire to act on what has been heard that arises from personal need rather than the client's need. Balancing the need for personal traumatic experiences to inform discourses of social justice needs constant discussion and review. The 'conversations of accountability' she describes can give a different nuance to supervision.

Life-cycle issues

Sensitivity to traumatic material changes over the professional life cycle. Sometimes this will coincide with significant personal life-cycle issues – important relationships ending; birth of a child; illness of a child; illness of a parent; personal illness; death of a significant other. Personal trauma memories can intertwine with those presented at work.

> I remember when I returned from maternity leave, I was allocated a new case. It was horrifying and involved serious physical and sexual abuse of a baby. I felt unable to talk about this with my colleagues, worried that they wouldn't see me as professional. I was also upset that no one considered the suitability of this case for me at the time.

Overwhelmed organisations

If one component of therapy is, as Flaskas (2005) says, the task of tolerating powerful emotions, then the challenge for supervision may be how to help supervisees position themselves to remain connected to emotion (even be moved by it) without being so overwhelmed by it that thinking or moving between levels of therapeutic discourse – from feelings to ideas recursively – becomes impossible. This ability will be seriously compromised if the wider organisational context is also overwhelmed.

Bloom and Farragher (2011) describe the process where systems become unbalanced and unable to process emotionally charged information. In a traumatised work system, chronically stressed and stretched to capacity dealing with highly emotive clinical issues, the system becomes increasingly 'amnesic' to its purpose and function and 'alexithymic' in relation to its workforce. This inability to process intense emotional experiences can lead to authoritarian and punitive management and supervision styles. This increases the likelihood of vicarious traumatisation.

In addition, chronic workplace stress limits new learning (Bloom and Farragher, 2011). It will inhibit clinicians from developing thoughtful clinical practice that includes testing hypotheses and will encourage working from positions of certainty and increasingly manualised approaches.

Flaskas (2002) points out that therapeutic impasse (the material often taken to supervision) require attention to be given to the clinician's emotional self. Traumatic material may be the least likely material to be brought. Rober (1999) refers to the therapeutic impasse as 'a paralysis of the circle of meaning of the outer conversation'. This process of paralysis can also occur within the supervisory context. In a chronically stressed workplace, the possibility of nurturing a conscious learning environment capable of thoughtful, compassionate practice becomes almost impossible.

Developing a supportive but challenging supervisory structure is essential to maintain the integrity of clinical practice. This needs to include an invitation to participate, be stretched and respond; to become an evolutionary systemic supervision – recursive, generative and reflexive without deleting the wider political context that shapes professional thoughts, feelings and actions.

Supervision as safe space for exploring unsafe issues

> This impossibility of expressing something in words may refer to the individual's impotence of capturing his/her experience in words (for example, in cases of traumatic experience), but it may also refer to the *unsafe dialogical context* in which the individual avoids talking because speaking openly can be dangerous for oneself or someone else (Baxter and Wilmot, 1985; Rober *et al.*, 2006)

Supervision needs to be a safe space and able to move into the potentially dangerous territory of trauma remembering dialogues. Current constructions regarding trauma are often very linear with defined perpetrators and victims, and with little interchange between these positions. At the other extreme the idea of 'competing narratives' emerges which smoothes over wider contextual and political issues that impact significantly on a particular interaction.

How do clinicians position themselves in the wider political arena? (Patel, 2007). This can feel like a provocative question. Perhaps perturbation and provocation to think differently and widely is helpful within healthy organisational contexts. The Just Therapy group have encouraged clinicians to actively consider their 'response abilities' (Fredman, 2004).

> As a family clinician I believe that I should cease to serve as a clinician when I become unwilling or unable to assume the position of activist. I do not believe that promoting the cause of human rights is inconsistent with helping couples and families ameliorate distress in their lives (Waldegrave and Tamasese, 1993).

Finding a way to keep responsibility for traumatic acts within a discourse of social justice without stifling curiosity and limiting therapeutic conversations is essential. Moving between different levels of context can help.

Competing narratives, as long as they remain in conversation with each other, can produce change. When they become frozen (Blow and Daniel, 2002) or monological, this can be the material brought to supervision. The 'avoidance of difference ... can masquerade as respect or non judgmental attitudes' (Reilly, 1999). Ethical principles need to guide clinicians toward required actions or practice.

In working with trauma, the clinician can also become 'idealised' by colleagues, 'sometimes glorifying our ability to be "so compassionate", "so robust"' (Patel, 2007, p. 236). This form of curiosity – 'How do you do it?' – is probably unhelpful as it is often not an invitation to open the discussion but more to close it down. 'I am glad YOU do it so I don't have to'.

In doing work with traumatic experiences across the life span, clinicians need to be 'ready to hear what clients bring' – their truth. To do this requires reflection on what constitutes a state of readiness. This is more than 'emotional presupposing' and 'postures of tranquillity' (Fredman, 2004). It includes an awareness of personal ideas and experiences that will influence and shape clinical work; revisiting the sources of inspiration for healing work; and finding new ones to fit with changing life circumstances/work contexts.

> ... I believed that systems concepts afforded me a language to communicate ideas that I failed to translate from their Buddhist or Taoist traditions. I kept the Buddhist and Taoist views very much to myself (as a South African of Lebanese Byzantine Catholic cultural background and Anglo/Teutonic descent, things were complicated enough) ... (Faris, 2002, p. 94).

Issues regarding race, gender, class and culture surface in clinical work all the time. This intersection of multiple aspects of identity can be fraught with contradictions. More aspects of self are being brought into the professional arena for public inspection. How do clinicians prepare to embody the working ethic? How can 'ordinary virtues' – maintenance of dignity, care for others, respect for moral standards and love of aesthetic pleasure (Todorov, 1990) be made visible in clinical practice?

Supervision as part of self-care

Resilience and emotional wellbeing need to be incorporated into the workplace and working practices. Supervision needs to be seen as part of the protective environment that makes working with traumatic material safer. Revisiting connections with family, community and culture, in its widest sense, through supervision, whilst maintaining a life-cycle approach to the supervision process seems essential.

Working with trauma can also promote personal growth and development (Arnold *et al.*, 2005). Having a supervision context to reflect on this, needs to be an essential part of professional emotional wellbeing and resilience. Developing and maintaining personal and professional self-care plans should be a priority (Carroll *et al.*, 1999, cited in Gilroy *et al.*, 2002). Common themes emerge when examining longevity and continued enjoyment of clinical practice (Dlugos and Friedlander, 2001, p. 301). These can be summarised as: a good work/personal life balance; a broad spectrum of clinical practice, including teaching, therapy, supervision and consultation; a wide range of client groups and treatment modalities; personal development work, including but not exclusively compassionate self care and a sense of the spiritual. While good supervision and engaging in personal therapy were considered helpful, personal and professional lifestyle choices were seen as most helpful (Dlugos and Friedlander, 2001, p. 301).

Conclusion

Recognising and acknowledging personal vulnerabilities and frailties can become a source of inspiration within our clinical practice (Cozolino, 2004). Connection is about hope – hope that no matter what has happened, no matter what we have done or what has been done to us, there are possibilities of transformation (McGoldrick and Hines, 2007, p. 59).

Traumatic experience is often an unworded emotional one, so making discourses of emotion, both in therapy and supervision, visible and audible is fundamentally important (Spellman and Smith, 2010). Conversation (and by implication supervision) is deemed 'therapeutic to the extent that it shows dialogical, rather than monological properties' (Guilfoyle, 2003, p. 332). Helping clinicians think about trauma work creatively is vital. In this regard, it is essential that supervisory practice instils hope and possibilities. It needs to honour the connections between people – the matrix of relationships each of equal importance, resonating recursively with salutogenic possibilities.

GLOSSARY

Affect regulation
This relates to the process of managing feelings. High emotional states like fear, anger or excitement subside as we learn to modulate and moderate these emotional highs. Developmentally this is learnt through the primary attachment figure, usually the mother. If exposed to stress chronically the capacity to manage and regulate affect becomes impaired because the neurobiological system becomes driven by the stress response.

Amygdala hijack
Based on research by Joseph Le Doux and popularised by Goleman (1996) 'the architecture of the brain gives the amygdala a privileged position as the emotional sentinel, able to hijack the brain'. The amygdala is our fear centre.

Commission to Inquire into Child Abuse (CICA)/Ryan Report
The Commission to Inquire into Child Abuse was set up by the Irish government to investigate the widespread abuse of children in Irish care facilities from 1936 onwards. It is commonly known as the Ryan Report after the judge who chaired the commission. It sat for 10 years and published its findings in May 2009.

Coordinated management of meaning (CMM)
This model sees communication as constitutive, and examines patterns of interaction, considering a variety of contexts and particularly the highest context at a given time.

Dialectical behaviour therapy (DBT)
This is a type of therapy developed by Marsha Linehan for working with borderline personality disordered clients. It combines cognitive behaviour therapy and relaxation techniques, including 'mindfulness', to help clients stabilise their mood and work on their symptoms.

Emotional freedom techniques (EFT)
A healing system devised by Gary Craig based on a sequence of tapping points. There has been considerable research on the technique in its original form. Gary Craig retired from public practice in June 2010. Originally a self-help technique easily available on the web, it is now more regulated. It is easily learned and has been shown to be effective in reducing stress and traumatic symptoms. See http://www. EFTuniverse.com/ (accessed 6 August 2012) for more information.

Emotional postures
The nonverbal messages that the clinician's body conveys to the client.

Emotional presupposing
Imagining the likely emotional flow of the therapeutic conversation before the session begins.

Eye movement desensitisation and reprocessing (EMDR)
Developed by Dr. Francine Shapiro. This type of treatment intervention has good clinical results in the treatment of trauma. See http://www.emdrassociation.org.uk/ (accessed 6 August 2012) for more information in the UK.

Externalisation
A systemic concept first introduced in the 1980s by Michael White and referring to the practice of seeing problems as external to the person, rather than part of them. See http://www.dulwichcentre.com.au/externalising.html (accessed 6 August 2012) for a detailed discussion.

Foresight project
Foresight projects are in depth studies on specific issues that have a wider social bearing. The Mental Capital and Wellbeing was one such project and the report was published in 2008. See http://www.bis.gov.uk/assets/bispartners/foresight/docs/mental-capital/mentalcapitalwellbeingexecsum.pdf (accessed 6 August 2012) for more information.

Hypothetical future questions
The focus on future possibilities, rather than past negatives, during therapy.

Mental Health Act
Refers to specific legislation in the UK regarding mental health and mental capacity. It covers circumstances where a person can be detained

in psychiatric provision without their consent. It covers definitions of mental disorder, professional roles, criteria for detention and other specific steps that ensure clarity in situations where someone is at risk to themself or others as a consequence of their mental health. http://www. legislation.gov.uk/ukpga/2007/12/contents (accessed 13 August 2012).

Mentalisation
The capacity to consider our own thoughts and feelings and imagine the thoughts and feelings of others. It is based on a theory of mind and connected to attachment ideas suggesting that we learn how to imagine other's thinking/feeling processes through our experience of someone's, usually our mother's, imagining and responding to our unspoken needs and affective states in early infancy.

Meta-communicate
Communicating about communicating. The idea originates with Bateson's theory of mind. Meta-communication considers messages given at different levels simultaneous which may require comment to clarify what the intended communication is.

Midbrain
The old part of the mammalian brain, sitting on top of the brain stem and effectively surrounded by the cortex. It is strongly associated with the fight or flight response and other strong emotional responses.

Neurophenomenology
A study developed by Varela which argued that our thoughts, beliefs and consciousness can only be understood in terms of the enactive structures in which they arise, namely the body (understood both as a biological system and as personally, phenomenologically experienced) and the physical world with which the body interacts.

National Institute for Health and Clinical Excellence (NICE)
The National Institute for Health and Clinical Excellence is an independent organisation that provides guidance, sets quality standards and manages a national database to improve people's health and prevent and treat ill health. http://www.nice.org.uk/aboutnice/ (accessed 6 August 2012).

Oyneg Shabes
A collective who coordinated a project dedicated to recording life in the Warsaw Ghetto during the Second World War Nazi-German occupation.

Pineal body
The pineal body is a midbrain structure responsible for the production of melatonin, a serotonin derivative. It sets our daily and seasonal rhythms. The pineal body has been seen as the seat of the soul or third eye.

Pituitary gland
The pituitary gland is a midbrain structure. In Kundalini yoga it is referred to as the master gland. It secretes nine hormones that regulate our body, including the stress hormone cortisol. It is strongly influenced by the hypothalamus, another midbrain structure.

Problem-saturated stories
This term comes from the narrative therapy of Michael White and David Epston. As the term implies, these stories focus on negative aspects of self which become defining, almost to the exclusion of other aspects of identity. Within a clinical setting it can be easy to become preoccupied with the problem-saturated story. However, to disregard the story completely may also be a disservice to your client.

Reframing
A technique in systemic therapy connected to Virginia Satir and Milton Erikson where a different 'frame' allows something to be viewed in a new way.

Relational risk
Barry Mason used this term in 2008 in respect of heterosexual men who had affairs and wished to resume their relationships with their long term partners. It refers to a preparedness to move into uncomfortable positions to explore ways of being with each other and through that journey moving into what Mason would term as 'safe uncertainty' – a context that allows the exploration of areas of discomfort.

Significant harm
This term refers to the threshold set by Section 31(10) of the UK Children Act 1989, which states that 'where the question of whether harm suffered by a child is significant turns on the child's health or development, his health or development shall be compared with that which could reasonably be expected of a similar child'.

Strategic therapy
This school of family therapy is based on Bateson's work into cybernetics.

Jay Haley is considered one of the main theorists of the approach. It is based on the idea that a problem persists because the solutions generated have repeatedly been ineffective and in turn become problematic themselves. It is focused on the here and now of lived experience and understands symptoms as a form of communication. Interventions often take a prescriptive form.

Survivor guilt
Where someone feels they should not have been spared from the traumatic experience.

Vicarious trauma
Where someone experiences overwhelming distress from witnessing the traumatisation of someone else.

REFERENCES

Alon, N. and Omer, H. (2006) *The Psychology of Demonization*. London: Lawrence Erlrbaum.

American Psychiatric Association (2000) *Diagnostic and Statistical Manual of Mental Disorders* (4th edition). Washington, DC.

Andersen, T. (1987) 'The Reflecting Team: Dialogue and Meta Dialogue in Clinical Work', *Family Process* 26, 415–28.

Andersen, T. (1997) 'Researching Client–Therapist Relationships: A Collaborative Study for Informing Therapy', *Journal of Systemic Therapies*, 16 (2), 125–33.

Anderson, H. and Goolishian, H. (1992) 'The Client is the Expert: A Not-knowing Approach to Therapy, in McNamee, S. and Gergen, K. J. (eds) *Therapy as Social Construction*, 25–39. London: Sage.

Andrews, B. and Brewin, C. (1990) 'Attributions of Blame for Marital Violence: A Study of Antecedents and Consequences', *Journal of Marriage and Family* 52 (3), 757–67.

Andrews, B., Brewin, C. R., Rose, S. and Kirk, M. (2000) 'Predicting PTSD Symptoms in Victims of Violent Crime: The Role of Shame, Anger, and Childhood Abuse', *Journal of Abnormal Psychology* 109, 69–73.

Arnold, D., Calhoun, L. G., Tedeschi, R. and Cann, A. (2005) 'Vicarious Posttraumatic Growth in Psychotherapy', *Journal of Humanistic Psychology* 45, 239–63.

Aston, M. and Rowley, T. (1974) *Landscape Archaeology: an Introduction to Fieldwork Techniques on Post-Roman Landscapes*. Newton Abbot: David & Charles.

Barbaro, B. de, Opoczyńska, M., Rostworowska, M., Drożdżowicz, L. and Golański, M. (2008) 'Changes in the Patient's Identity in the Context of a Psychiatric System – An Empirical Study', *Journal of Family Therapy* 30, 438–49.

Barge, K. (2004) 'Articulating CMM as a Practical Theory', in Pearce, W. B. and Kearney, J. (eds) *Human Systems*, Volume 15 (1–3).

Baruch, V. (2004) 'Self-Care for Therapists: Prevention of Compassion Fatigue and Burnout', *Psychotherapy in Australia* 10 (4), 64–8.

Bateson, G. (1973) *Steps to an Ecology of Mind*. London: Paladin,

Bateson, G. and Bateson, M. C. (1987) *Angels Fear: Towards an Epistemology of the Sacred*. New York: Macmillan.

Baxter, L. and Wilmot, W. (1985) 'Taboo Topics in Close Relationships', *Journal of Social and Personal Relationships* 2 (3), 253–69.

Bentall, R. P. (2009) *Doctoring the Mind: Why Psychiatric Treatments Fail*. London: Allen Lane.

Berger, M. (2007) 'New NHS clinical Information Systems: The challenge of Diagnosis and Other Issues', *Clinical Psychology Forum* 179 Nov., 19–23.

Bertrando, P. (2007) *The Dialogical Therapist*. London: Karnac.

Bertrando, P. and Gilli, G. (2008) 'Emotional Dances: Therapeutic Dialogues as Embodied Systems', *Journal of Family Therapy* 30, 362–73.

Bifulco, A., Harris, T. and Brown, G. W. (1992) 'Mourning or Early Inadequate Care?', *Development and Psychopathology* 4, 433–49.

Bloom, S. (1997) *Creating Sanctuary: Toward the Evolution of Sane Societies*. New York: Routledge.

Bloom, S. and Farragher, B. (2011) *Destroying Sanctuary: The Crisis in Human Services Delivery*. Oxford: Oxford University Press.

Blow, K. and Daniel, G. (2002) 'Frozen Narratives? Post Divorce Processes and Contact Disputes', *Journal of Family Therapy* 24 (1), 85–103.

Borossa, J. (ed) (1999) *Selected Writings: Sandor Ferenczi*. London: Penguin.

Boscolo, L., Cecchin, G., Hoffman, L. and Penn, P. (1987) *Milan Systemic Family Therapy: Conversations in Theory and Practice*. New York: Basic Books.

Boscolo, L. and Bertrando, P. (1992) 'The Reflexive Loop of Past, Present, and Future in Systemic Therapy and Consultation', *Family Process* 31, 119–30.

Boston, P. (2000) 'Systemic Family Therapy and the Influence of Post-modernism', *Advances in Psychiatric Treatment* (2000) 6, 450–7.

Boyle, M. (2006) 'From "Schizophrenia" to "Psychosis": Paradigm Shift or More of the Same?', paper presented to the Division of Clinical Psychology Annual Conference, London, December 2006.

Bradley, S. J. (2000) *Affect Regulation and the Development of Psychopathology*. New York: Guilford.

Bray, M. and Kane, F. (2006) Tblisi State Conservatory No. 4 Bulletin, June 2006, Ethnomusicology 'What Trauma has Destroyed, Conscious Vibration Can Rebuild: A New Role for Georgian Singing, or the Continuation of its Ancient Function?' http://www.statetheta.com/docs/georgian/ethnomusicology.pdf (accessed 8 August 2012).

Brewin, C. (2007) 'Remembering and Forgetting', in Friedman, M., Keane, T. and Resick, P. (eds) *Handbook of PTSD: Science and Practice*, 116–34. London: Guilford Press.

Byrne, N. and McCarthy, I. (2007) 'The Dialectical Structure of Hope and Despair: A Fifth Province Approach', in Flaskas, C., McCarthy, I. and Sheehan, J. (eds) *Hope and Despair in Narrative Family Therapy: Adversity, Forgiveness and Reconciliation*, 36–49. London: Routledge.

Burck, C. and Campbell, D. (2002) 'Training Systemic Supervisors: Multilayered Learning', in Campbell, D. and Mason, B. (eds) *Perspectives in Supervision*, 59–80. London: Karnac.

Burck, C., Hildebrand, J. and Mann, J. (1996) 'Women's Tales: Systemic Groupwork with Mothers Post-separation', *Journal of Family Therapy* 18, 163–82.

Burnham, J. (1992) 'Approach–Method–Technique: Making Distinctions and Creating Connections', *Human Systems* 3, 3–27.

Burnham, J. (1993) 'Systemic Supervision: The Evolution of Reflexivity in the Context of the Supervisory Relationship', *Human Systems* 4, 349–81.

Burnham, J. and Harris, Q. (2002) 'Cultural Issues in Supervision', in Campbell, D. and Mason, B. (eds) *Perspectives on Supervision*. London: Karnac.

Burnham, J., Palma, D. A. and Whitehouse, L. (2008) 'Learning as a Context for Differences and Differences as a Context for Learning', *Journal of Family Therapy* 30, 529–42.

Byng-Hall, J.(1980) 'Symptom Bearer as Marital Distance Regulator: Clinical Implications', *Family Process* 19, 355–65.

Cairns, K. (2010) *Circles of Harm: Surviving Paedophilia and Network Abuse* (2nd edition). London: Lonely Scribe.

Carr, A. (2000a) 'Michael White's Narrative Therapy, in Carr, A. (ed) *Clinical psychology in Ireland , Volume 4 Family Therapy Theory, Practice and Research 9*, 15–38. Lampeter: Edwin Mellen Press.

Carr, A. (2000b) *Family Therapy: Concepts, Process and Practice*. London: Wiley.

Cecchin, G. (1987) 'Hypothesizing, Circularity and Neutrality Revisited: An Invitation to Curiosity', *Family Process* 26, 405–13.

Cecchin, G., Lane, G. and Ray, W. (1994) *The Cybernetics of Prejudices in the Practice of Psychotherapy*. London: Karnac

Commission to Inquire into Child Abuse Report (CICA) (also known as The Ryan Report) (2009) http://www.childabusecommission.ie/ (accessed 8 August 2012).

Corey, G. (2009) *Case Approach to Counselling and Psychotherapy* (7th edition). Belmont, CA: Brooks/Cole.

Cozolino, L. (2004) *The Making of a Therapist: A Practical Guide for the Inner Journey*. New York: WW Norton & Co.

Cronen, V. E. (2001) 'Practical Theory, Practical Art, and the Pragmatic-systemic Account of Inquiry', *Communication Theory*, Volume 11, 1, 14–35.

Cronen, V. E. and Pearce, W. B. (1980) *Communication, Action and Meaning*. New York: Praeger.

Dallos, R. and Urry, A. (1999) 'Abandoning our Parents and Grandparents: Does Social Construction Mean the End of Systemic Family Therapy?', *Journal of Family Therapy* 21(2), 161–86.

Daly, M. (1978) *Gyn/Ecology: The Metaethics of Radical Feminism*. London: The Women's Press.

Delbo, C. (2010) *Témoigner entre histoire et mémoire, No. 105*. Editions Kimé.

Denborough, D. (ed) (2006) *Trauma: Narrative Responses to Traumatic Experience*. Adelaide: Dulwich Centre.

Denborough, D. (2008) *Collective Narrative Practice: Responding to Individuals, Groups and Communities who have Experienced Trauma*. Adelaide: Dulwich Centre.

Dimeff, L. and Linehan, M. M. (2001) 'Dialectical Behavior Therapy in a Nutshell', *The Californian Psychologist* 34, 10–13.

Dlugos, R. F. and Friedlander, M. L. (2001) 'Passionately Committed

Psychotherapists: A Qualitative Study of Their Experiences', *Professional Psychology: Research and Practice*, Vol. 32 (3), 298–304.

Dowling, E. and Gorell Barnes, G. (1999) *Working with Children and Parents through Separation and Divorce: The Changing Lives of Children*. London: Palgrave.

Draper, R. and Dallos, R. (2010) *An Introduction to Family Therapy: Systemic Theory and Practice* (3rd edition). Maidenhead: Open University Press.

Emerson, D. and Hopper, E. (2011) *Overcoming Trauma Through Yoga: Reclaiming Your Body*. Berkeley, CA: North Atlantic.

Epston, D. and White, M. (1992) *Experience, Contradiction, Narrative and Imagination*. Adelaide: Dulwich Centre.

Faris, J. (2002) 'Some Reflections on Process, Relationship and Personal Development in Supervision', in Campbell, D. and Mason, B. (eds) *Practice of Supervision*. London: Karnac.

Felitti, V. J. *et al.* (1998) 'Relationship of Childhood Abuse and Household Dysfunction to Many of the Leading Causes of Death in Adults. The Adverse Childhood Experiences (ACE) Study', *American Journal of Preventative Medicine* 14 (4), 245–58.

Figley, C. (1995) *Compassion Fatigue: Coping with Secondary Traumatic Stress Disorder in Those Who Treat the Traumatized*. New York: Brunner Mazel.

Firestone, S. (1979) *The Dialectic of Sex: The Case for Feminist Revolution*. London: The Women's Press.

Fisch, R., Weakland, J. H. and Segal, L. (1982) *The Tactics of Change: Doing Therapy Briefly*. San Francisco: Jossey Bass.

Fishbane, M. D. (2007) 'Wired to Connect: Neuroscience, Relationships, and Therapy', *Family Process* 46, 395–412.

Flaskas, C. (1997) 'Engagement and the Therapeutic Relationship in Family Therapy', *Journal of Family Therapy* 9, 263–82.

Flaskas, C. (2002) *Family Therapy Beyond Post Modernism: Practice Challenges Theory*. Hove: Brunner.

Flaskas (2005) 'Sticky Situations, Therapy Mess: On Impasse and Reflective Practice', in Flaskas, C., Mason, B. and Perlesz, A. (eds) *The Space Between: Experience, Context and Process in the Therapeutic Relationship*. London: Karnac.

Flemons, D. (1991) *Completing Distinctions: Interweaving the Ideas of Gregory Bateson and Taoism Into a Unique Approach to Therapy*. London: Shambhala.

Folman, A. (2008) *Waltz with Bashir* (film).

Fonagy, P. and Target, M. (1996) 'Playing With Reality: I. Theory Of Mind And The Normal Development of Psychic Reality', *International Journal of Psycho-Analysis* 77, 217–33.

Foresight Mental Capital and Wellbeing Project (2008) Final Project Report – Executive Summary. *Mental Capital and Wellbeing: Making the Most of Ourselves in the 21st Century*. London: The Government Office for Science.

Fox, H., Tench, C. and Marie (2002) 'Outsider Witness Practices and Group Supervision', International Journal of Narrative Therapy and Community Work, No. 4.

Frame, M. W. (2000) 'The Spiritual Genogram in Family Therapy', *Journal of Marital and Family Therapy* 26, 211–16.

Frankl, V. (2011) *Man's Search For Meaning: The Classic Tribute to Hope from the Holocaust*. Reading: Rider.

Fredman, G. (2004) *Transforming Emotion: Conversations in Counselling and Psychotherapy*. London: Whurr.

Fredman, G. (2007) 'Preparing Our Selves for the Therapeutic Relationship. Revisiting "Hypothesizing Revisited"', *Human Systems* 18, 44–59.

Friedman, M., Keane, T. and Resick, P. (eds) (2007) *Handbook of PTSD: Science and Practice*. London: Guilford.

Friedman, S. (ed) (1995) *The Reflecting Team in Action: Collaborative Practice in Family Therapy*. London: Guilford.

Frosh, S. (1997) 'Fundamentalism, Gender and Family Therapy', *Journal of Family Therapy* 19, 417–30.

Fruggeri, L. (2002) 'Different Levels of Analysis in the Supervisory Process', in Campbell, D. and Mason, B. (eds) *Practice of Supervision*. London: Karnac.

Gergen, K. (1990) 'Affect and Organization in Postmodern Society', in Srivastva, S. and Cooperrider, D. L. (eds) *Appreciative Management and Leadership*, 153–74. San Francisco: Jossey Bass.

Gergen, K. (2001) *Social Construction in Context*. London: Sage.

Gergen, K. (2009) *An Invitation to Social Construction* (2nd edition). London: Sage.

Gergen, M. and Gergen, K. (2010) 'Afterwords: Working with Elders: Inspiring the Young', in Fredman, G., Anderson E. and Stott, J. (eds) *Being with Older People: A Systemic Approach*, 257–62. London: Karnac.

Gil, E. (1996) *Treating Abused Adolescents*. London: Guilford

Gilroy, P. J., Carroll, L. and Murra, J. (2002) 'A Preliminary Survey of Counseling Psychologists' Personal Experiences With Depression and Treatment', *Professional Psychology: Research and Practice* 33 (4), August 2002, 402–7.

Goldner, V., Penn, P., Sheinberg, M. and Walker, G. (1990) 'Love and Violence: Gender Paradoxes in Volatile Attachments', *Family Process* 29, 343–64.

Goldstein, E. (2010) 'Mindfulness and Trauma: An Interview with John Briere', PsychCentral, http://blogs.psychcentral.com/mindfulness/2010/03/mindfulness-and-trauma-an-interview-with-john-briere—ph-d/ (accessed 8 August 2012).

Goleman, D. (1996) *Emotional Intelligence: Why It Can Matter More Than IQ*. London: Bloomsbury.

Gorell Barnes, G. (1999) 'Operationalizing the Uncertain: Some Clinical Reflections', *Journal of Family Therapy* 21, 145–53.

Gourevitch, P. (2009) 'People's Hearts and Minds Need Time to Heal', *The Observer Magazine*, 8 November 2012, 34.

Gradus, J. L. *et al.* (2010) 'Posttraumatic Stress Disorder and Completed Suicide', *American Journal of Epidemiology* 171, 721–7.

Griffith, J. L. and Griffith, M. (1994) *The Body Speaks: Therapeutic Dialogues for Mind–Body Problems*. New York: Basic Books.

Groen, M. and Van Lawick, J. (2009) *Intimate Warfare: Regarding the Fragility of Family Relations*. London: Karnac.

Guilfoyle, M. (2003) 'Dialogue and Power: A Critical Analysis of Power in Dialogical Therapy', *Family Process* 42 (3), 331–43.

Haley, J. (1973) *Uncommon Therapy*. New York: W. W. Norton.

Haley, J. (1987) *Problem Solving Therapy*. San Franciso: Jossey Bass.

Haney, C., Banks, C. and Zimbardo, P. (1973) 'Interpersonal Dynamics in a Simulated Prison', *International Journal of Criminology and Penology* 1, 67–9.

Harré, R. (1997) 'Are Emotions Significant in Psychology only as Motives?', *Journal for the Theory of Social Behaviour* 27, 503–5.

Hartman, C. R. and Jackson, H. (1994) 'Rape and the Phenomenon of Countertransference', in J. P. Wilson and J. D. Lindy (eds) *Countertransference in the Treatment of PTSD*, 206–44. New York: Guilford.

Hawkins, P. and Shohet, R. (2007) *Supervision in the Helping Professions*. Berkshire, UK: McGraw-Hill.

Healey, A. (2004) 'A Different Description of Trauma: A Wider Systemic Perspective – A Personal Insight', *Journal of Child Care in Practice* 10, 167–84.

Hedges, F. (2005) *An Introduction to Systemic Therapy with Individuals: A Social Constructionist Approach*. London: Palgrave.

Herman, J. L. (1997) *Trauma and Recovery: The Aftermath of Violence from Domestic Abuse to Political Terror* (previous edition: 1992). New York: Basic Books.

Hermans, H. J. M. and Dimaggio, G. (2007) 'Self, Identity, and Globalization in Times of Uncertainty: A Dialogical Analysis', *Review of General Psychology* 11, 31–61.

Himle, D., Jayaratne, S. and Thyness, P. (1989) 'The Buffering Effects of Four Types of Supervisory Support on Work Stress', *Administration in Social Work* 13, 19–35.

Hunter, M. (2009) 'Poor Supervision Continues to Hinder Child Protection Practice', *Community Care*, 22 April, http://www.communitycare.co.uk/Articles/21/04/2009/111339/exclusive-survey-reveals-social-work-burnout-fears.htm (accessed 8 August 2012).

Imber Black, E. (1998) *The Secret Life of Families: Truth-Telling, Privacy, and Reconciliation in a Tell-All Society*. London: Bantam.

International Statistical Classification of Diseases and Related Health Problems (ICD) (2007) 10th Revision Version. Geneva: World Health Organisation.

James, K. (2007) 'The Interactional Process of Forgiveness and Responsibility: A Critical Assessment of Family Therapy Literature', in Flaskas, C., McCarthy, I. and Sheehan, J. (eds) *Hope and Despair in Narrative Family Therapy: Adversity, Forgiveness and Reconciliation*, 127–39. London: Routledge.

Jenmorri, K. (2006) 'Of Rainbows and Tear: Exploring Hope and Despair in Trauma Therapy', *Child and Youth Care Forum* 35 (1), 41–55.

Jones, E. (2007) 'Moving On: Forgiveness, Vengeance and Reconciliation', in Flaskas, C., McCarthy, I. and Sheehan, J. (eds) *Hope and Despair in Narrative Family Therapy:Adversity, Forgiveness and Reconciliation*, 150–61. London: Routledge.

Kabat-Zinn, J. (1991) *Full Catastrophe Living: Using the Wisdom of Your Body and Mind to Face Stress, Pain, and Illness*. New York: Delacorte.

Kassow, S. D. (2007) *Who Will Write Our History*. London: Penguin.

Kavner, E. and McNab, S. (2005) 'Therapist experience of shame', in Flaskas, C., Mason, B. and Perlesz, A. (eds) *The Space Between: Experience, Context and Process in the Therapeutic Relationship*, 141–56. London: Karnac.

Kearney, J. (2004) 'Glossary', *Human Systems* 15, 7–10.

Kilminster, S. M. and Jolly, B. C. (2000) 'Effective Supervision in Clinical Practice Settings: A Literature Review', *Medical Education* 34 (10), 827–40.

Lang, P. and McAdam, E. (1997) 'Narrative-Acting: Future Dreams in Present Living: Jottings on an Honouring Theme', *Human Systems* 8 (1), 3–12.

Larner, G. (1994) 'Para-Modern Family Therapy: Deconstructing Post-modernism', *Australian and New Zealand Journal of Family Therapy* 15, 11–16.

Layne, C. M., Warren, J. S., Watson, P. J. and Shalev, A. Y. (2007) 'Risk, Vulnerabilities, Resistance and Resilience: Towards Integrated Conceptualization of Posttraumatic Adaptation', in Friedman, Matthew; Keane, T. and Resick, P. (eds.) (2007) *Handbook of PTSD: Science and Practice*, 497–520. London: Guilford Press.

Lee, L. and Littlejohns, S. (2006) 'Deconstructing Agnes: Externalization in Systemic Supervision', *Journal of Family Therapy* 29 (3), 238–48.

Levine, P. (1997) *Waking the Tiger: Healing Trauma – The Innate Capacity to Transform Overwhelming Experiences*. Berkeley, CA: North Atlantic.

Levy, A. and Scott–Clark, C. (2010) 'Death of a Child', *The Guardian*, 6 February 2010.

Liddle, H. A. and Saba, G. S. (1983) 'On Context Replication: The Isomorphic Relationship of Training and Therapy', *Journal of Strategic and Systemic Therapies* 2, 3–11.

Liddle, H. A. (1988) 'Systemic Supervision: Conceptual Overlays and Pragmatic Guidelines', in Liddle, H. L., Breulin, D. C. and Schwartz, R. C. (eds) *Handbook of Family Therapy* Vol. 2, 638–97. New York: Bruner/Mazel.

Llosa, C. (2009) *The Milk of Sorrow* [Spanish: *La Teta Asustda*].

Lowenstein, S., Reder, P. and Clark, A. (1982) 'The Consumers' Response: Trainees Discussion of the Experience of Live Supervision', in Byng-Hall, J. and Whiffen, R. (eds) *Family Therapy Supervision*, 115–29. London: Academic.

Lyotard, J.-F. (1984) *The Postmodern Condition: A Report on Knowledge*. Minneapolis: University of Minnesota Press.

MacFarlane, A. C. (1997) 'The Prevalence and Longitudinal Course of PTSD', *Annals of the New York Academy of Sciences* 821, 10–23.

Madanes, C. (1982) *Strategic Family Therapy*. San Francisco, CA: Jossey-Bass.

Madigan, S. (2007) 'Anticipating Hope Within Written and Naming Domains of Despair', in Flaskas, C., McCarthy, I. and Sheehan, J. (eds) *Hope and Despair in Narrative and Family Therapy*, 100–13. London: Routledge.

Mason, B. (1993) 'Towards Positions of Safe Uncertainty', *Human Systems* 4, 189–200.

Mason, B. (2005) 'Relational Risk Taking and the Training of Supervisors', *Journal of Family Therapy* 27 (3), 289–97.

Masters, B. (2012) 'Literally – The Much Misused Word of the Moment', *The Guardian*, 29 January 2012.

Maturana, H. R. and Varela, F. J. (1980) *Autopoiesis and Cognition. The Realization of the Living*. Dordrecht: Reidel.

McCrone, P. R., Knapp, M. R. J. and Cawkill, P. (2003) *Posttraumatic Stress Disorder (PTSD) in the Armed Forces: Health Economic Considerations* [online]. London: LSE Research Online.

McGoldrick, M. (1982) 'Through the Looking Glass: Supervision of a Trainee's Trigger Family', in Byng-Hall, J. and Whiffen, R. (eds.) *Family Therapy Supervision*. London: Academic.

McGoldrick, M. and Hines, P. (2007) 'Hope: The Far Side of Despair', in Flaskas, C., McCarthy, I. and Sheehan, J. (eds) *Hope and Despair in Narrative and Family Therapy*. London: Routledge.

McLean, S. and Wade, T. (2003) 'The Contribution of Therapist Beliefs to Psychological Distress in Therapists: An Investigation of Vicarious Traumatization, Burnout and Symptoms of Avoidance and Intrusion', *Behavioural and Cognitive Psychotherapy* 31, 417–28.

McNally, R. J. (2009) 'Can we Fix PTSD in DSM V?', *Depression and Anxiety* 26, 597–600.

McNally, R. J. (2010) 'Can we Salvage the Concept of Psychological Trauma?', *The Psychologist* 23 (5), 386–88.

Meltzer, H. *et al.* (2003) *The Mental Health of Young People Looked After by Local Authorities in England*. London: The Stationary Office.

Meltzer, H. (2005) 'The Prevalence of Mental Health and Mental Disorders in Childhood and Adolescence', in Williams, R. and Kerfoot, M. (eds) *Child and Adolescent Mental Health Services: Strategy, Planning, Delivery and Evaluation*. Oxford: Oxford University Press.

Minuchin, S. and Fishman, H. C. (1981) *Family Therapy Techniques*. Cambridge, MA: Harvard University Press.

Mollon, P. (2008) *Psychoanalytic Energy Psychotherapy*. London: Karnac.

Morgan, A. (2000) *What is Narrative Therapy? An Easy-to-Read Introduction*. Adelaide: Dulwich Centre.

Morrison, A. P., Frame, L. and Larkin, W. (2003) 'Relationships Between Trauma and Psychosis: A Review and Integration', *British Journal of Clinical Psychology* 42, 331–53.

Morrison, T. (1990) 'The Emotional Effects of Child Protection Work on the Worker' NISW/BASW paper first presented to BASPCAN Conference April 1990.

Morrison, T. (2005) *Staff Supervision in Social Care: Making a Real Difference for Staff and Service Users*. Brighton: Pavilion.

Mosley, T. and Wiewel, B. (2011) 'Trauma Focused Clinical Supervision: Building Trauma Competence in Our Workforce', http://www.uclaisap.org/slides/psattc/cod/2011/Workshop%20P%20-%20Wiewel-Mosley/clinical%20supervision%20notes%20oct%202011.pdf (accessed 8 August 2012).

Mullet, E. and Girard, M. (2000) 'Developmental and cognitive points of view on forgiveness', in McCullough, M. E., Pargement, K. I. and Thoreson, C. E. (eds) *Forgiveness: Theory, Research and Practice*. New York: Guilford.

Mullan, J. (2007) 'One Day at a Time', *The Guardian*, 17 March 2007.

National Institute of Clinical Excellence (NICE) (2005) *Clinical Guideline 26, Post-Traumatic Stress Disorder (PTSD): The Management of PTSD in Adults and Children in Primary and Secondary Care*. London: NICE.

National Strategic Framework for Aboriginal and Torres Strait Islander Health 2003–2012 (2007). http://www.health.gov.au/internet/main/publishing.nsf/

Content/6CA5DC4BF04D8F6ACA25735300807403/$File/nsfatsih2013.pdf (accessed 13 August 2012).

Norcross, J. C. (2000) 'Psychotherapist Self-Care: Practitioner-Tested, Research-Informed Strategies', *Professional Psychology: Research and Practice* 31(6), 710–13.

Norcross, J. C. and Guy, J. D. (2007) *Leaving it at the Office: A Guide to Psychotherapist Self-Care*. New York: Guilford.

Norris, F. and Slone, L. (2007) 'The Epidemiology of Trauma and PTSD', in Friedman, M. Keane, T. and Resick, P. (eds) *Handbook of PTSD: Science and Practice*, 78–98. London: Guilford.

Ogden, P. and Minton, K. (2000) 'Sensorimotor Psychotherapy: One Method for Processing Traumatic Memory', *Traumatology* 6(3), article 3.

Ogden, P., Minton, K. and Pain, C. (2006) *Trauma and the Body: A Sensorimotor Approach to Psychotherapy*. London: Norton.

Omer, H. (2000) *Parental Presence: Reclaiming a Leadership Role in Bringing up our Children*. Phoenix, AZ: Zeig, Tucker *et al.*

Otto, M. W. *et al.* (2007) 'Posttraumatic Stress Disorder Symptoms Following Media Exposure to Tragic Events: Impact of 9/11 on Children at Risk for Anxiety Disorders', *Journal of Anxiety Disorders* 21 (7), 888–902.

Owen, C. (2010) *Living with Evil*. London: Headline.

Ozer, E. J., Best, S. R., Lipsey, T. L. and Weiss, D. S. (2003) 'Predictors of Posttraumatic Stress Disorder and Symptoms in Adults: A Meta-Analysis', *Psychology Bulletin* 129 (1), 52–73.

Papadopoulos, R. (2002) *Therapeutic Care for Refugees. No Place Like Home*. London: Karnac.

Papadopoulos, R. (2007) 'Refugees, Trauma and Adversity-Activated Development', *European Journal of Psychotherapy and Counselling* 9 (3).

Papadopoulos, R. and Hildebrand, J. (1997) 'Is Home Where The Heart Is? Narratives of Oppositional Discourses in Refugee Families', in Papadopoulos, R. and Byng-Hall, J. (eds) *Multiple Voices: Narrative in Systemic Family Psychotherapy*, 206–36. London: Duckworth.

Patel, N. (2007) 'The Prevention of Torture: A Role for Clinical Psychologists', Journal of Critical Psychology, Counselling and Psychotherapy 7, 229–47.

Pearce, W. B. (2007) *Making Social Worlds: A Communication Perspective*. Oxford: Blackwell.

Pearlman, L. A. and Saakvitne, K. W. (1995) *Trauma and the Therapist: Countertransference and Vicarious Traumatization in Psychotherapy with Incest Survivors*. New York: W. W. Norton.

Qassim, A. (2007) 'Broken Bonds', *Guardian*, 4 August 2007, 3.

Read, J., Agar, K., Argyle, N. and Aderhold, V. (2003) 'Sexual and Physical Abuse During Childhood and Adulthood as Predictors of Hallucinations, Delusions and Thought Disorder', *Psychology and Psychotherapy: Theory Research and Practice* 76, 1–22.

Reilly, I. (1999) 'We Build to Fill the Centuries' Arrears', *Journal of Family Therapy* 21, 230–7.

Resnick, H. S. *et al.* (1993) 'Prevalence of Civilian Trauma and Posttraumatic

Stress Disorder in a Representative National Sample of Women', *Journal of Consulting and Clinical Psychology* 61, 984–91.

Ricoeur. P. (1999) 'Forgetting and the Difficulty of Forgiving', in Flaskas, C., McCarthy, I. and Sheehan, J. (eds) *Hope and Despair in Narrative and Family Therapy*. London: Routledge.

Rieff, D. (2007) 'The Militant Reader', *The Guardian*, 17 March 2007.

Rivers, W. H. R. (1918) 'The Repression of War Experience', *The Lancet* http://www.gwpda.org/comment/rivers.htm (accessed 8 August 2012).

Rivett, M. and Rees, A. (2004) 'Dancing on a Razor's Edge: Systemic Group Work with Batterers', *Journal of Family Therapy* 26, 142–62.

Rivett, M. and Rees, A. (2008) 'Firing Up and Burning Out: The Personal and Professional Impact of Working in Domestic Violence Offender Programmes', *Probation Journal* 55, 139–52.

Rober, P. (1999) 'The Therapist's Inner Conversation: Some Ideas About the Self of the Therapist, Therapeutic Impasse and the Process of Reflection', *Family Process* 38, 209–28.

Rober, P. (2005) 'The Therapist's Self in Dialogical Family Therapy', *Family Process* 44, 477–95.

Rober, P., Van Eesbeek, D. and Elliott, R. (2006) 'Talking About Violence: A Micro-Analysis of Narrative Processes in a Family Therapy Session', *Journal of Marital and Family Therapy* 32, 313–28.

Rober, P. and Seltzer, M. (2010) 'Avoiding Colonizer Positions in the Therapy Room: Some Ideas About the Challenges of Dealing with the Dialectic of Misery and Resources in Families', *Family Process* 49, 123–37.

Rose, A. J. (2002) 'Co-Rumination in the Friendships of Girls and Boys', *Child Development* 73, 1830–43.

Rose, A. J., Carlson, W. and Waller, E. M. (2007) 'Prospective Associations of Co-rumination with Friendship and Emotional Adjustment: Considering the Socioemotional Trade-offs of Co-rumination', *Developmental Psychology* July 43 4, 1019–31.

Rosenblatt (2000) http://www.pbs.org/newshour/essays/may00/rosenblatt_5-2.html (accessed 14 August 2012).

Rosenhan, D. (1973) 'On Being Sane in Insane Places', *Science* (American Association for the Advancement of Science) 179 (4070), 250–8.

Rostworowska, M., Opocznska, M. and de Barbaro, B. (2005) 'Systems Consultation: Opportunities and Limitations', *Archives of Psychiatry and Psychotherapy* 7, 43–9.

Roth, A. and Fonagy, P. (2004) *What Works for Whom? A Critical Review of Psychotherapy Research* (2nd edition). New York: Guilford.

Rothschild, B. (2000) *The Body Remembers: The Psychophysiology of Trauma and Trauma Treatment.* New York: Norton Professional.

Rutter, M. (1999) 'Resilience Concepts and Findings: Implications for Family Therapy', *Journal of Family Therapy* 21, 119–44.

Salecl, R. (2000) 'Why One Would Pretend to be a Victim of the Holocaust', *Other Voices* vol. 2, n. 1.

Schön, D. (1987) *Educating the Reflective Practitioner. Toward a New Design for Teaching and Learning in the Professions.* San Francisco: Jossey Bass.

Schön, D. (1983) *The Reflective Practitioner: How Professionals Think in Action.* New York: Basic Books.

Schore, A. (2002) 'Dysregulation of the Right Brain: A Fundamental Mechanism of Traumatic Attachment and the Psychopathogenesis of Posttraumatic Stress Disorder', *Australian and New Zealand Journal of Psychiatry* 36, 9–30.

Schore, A. (2003a) *Affect Regulation and the Repair of the Self.* London: Norton.

Schore, A. (2003b) *Affect Dysregulation and Disorders of the Self.* London: Norton.

Selekman, M. (1997) *Solution-Focused Therapy with Children: Harnessing Family Strengths for Systemic Change.* New York: Guilford.

Selvini Palazzoli, M. (1988) *Family Games: General Models of Psychotic Process in the Family.* New York: W. W. Norton.

Selvini Palazzoli, M., Boscolo, L., Cecchin, G., and Prata, G. (1980) 'Hypothesizing–Circularity–Neutrality: Three Guidelines for the Conductor of the Session', *Family Process* 19, 73–85.

Sheehan, J. (2007) 'Forgiveness and the Unforgivable: The Resurrection of Hope in Family Therapy', in Flaskas, C., McCarthy, I. and Sheehan, J. (eds) *Hope and Despair in Narrative and Family Therapy*, 161–73. London: Routledge.

Shepherd, B. (2004) 'Risk Factors and PTSD', in Rosen, G. (ed) *Posttraumatic Stress Disorder*, 39–61. Chichester: Wiley.

Shotter, J. (1993) *Conversational Realities: Constructing Life Through Language.* London: Sage.

Shragai, N. (2007) 'First Person Interview', *The Guardian*, 15 December 2007.

Siegel, D. (1999) *The Developing Mind: How Relationships and the Brain Interact to Shape Who We Are.* London: Guilford.

Siegel, D. and Hartzell, M. (2003) *Parenting from the Inside Out.* London: Penguin.

Sluzki, C. E. (1992) 'Transformations: A Blueprint for Narrative Changes in Therapy', *Family Process* 31(3), 217–30.

Sluzki, C. E. (2008) '"The Ancient Cult of Madame": When Therapists Trade Curiosity for Certainty', *Journal of Family Therapy* 30, 117–28.

Smith, G. (1987) (paper withdrawn) 'Child Sexual Abuse: Towards A Feminist Professional Practice' Report of the Conference Held by The Child Abuse Studies Unit, 6,7 and 8 April 1987 at The Polytechnic of North London, Edited by Mary MacLeod and Esther Saraga.

Smith, G. (1994) 'Parent, Partner, Protector: Conflicting Role Demands for Mothers of Children Who Have Been Sexually Abused', in Morrison, T., Beckett, R. and Erooga, M. (eds) *Sexual Offending Against Children: Assessment and Treatment of Male Abusers.* London: Routledge.

Smith, G. (1999) 'Resilience Concepts and Findings: Implications for Family Therapy', *Journal of Family Therapy* 21, 154–8.

Smith, G. (2005a) 'Constructions of Childhood', in Newnes, C. and Radcliffe, N. (eds) *Making and Breaking Children's Lives*, 3–15. Ross on Wye: PCCS.

Smith, G. (2005b) 'Children's Narratives of Traumatic Experiences', in Vetere, A. and Dowling, E. (eds) *Narrative Therapies with Children and Their Families: A Practitioners Guide to Concepts and Approaches.* London: Routledge.

Smith, G. (2008) *The Protectors' Handbook: Reducing the Risk of Child Sexual Abuse and Helping Children Recover.* London: British Association for Adopting and Fostering.

Smith, G. and Lewis, S. (Unpublished) 'Self Soothing Programme: Managing Everyday and Extraordinary Stress', Therapist Resource Pack.

Solomon, M. and Siegel, D. (eds) (2003) *Healing Trauma: Attachment, Mind, Body, and Brain*. New York: W. W. Norton.

Somasundaram, D. (2007) 'Collective Trauma in Northern Sri Lanka: A Qualitative Psychosocial-Ecological Study', *International Journal of Mental Health* Systems 1, 5.

Sontag, S. (2003) *Regarding the Pain of Others*. London: Penguin.

Spellman, D. and Smith, G. (2010) 'Three Gasps behind the Screen: Exploring Discourses of Emotion in Systemic Supervision', in Daniel, G. and Burck, C. (eds) *Mirrors and Reflections: Processes of Systemic Supervision*, 79–103. London: Karnac.

Storm, C. L., Todd, T. C., Sprenkle, D. H. and Morgan, M. M. (2001) 'Gaps Between MFT Supervision Assumptions and Common Practice: Suggested Best Practices', *Journal of Marital and Family Therapy* 27, 227–39.

Stratton, P. (2003) 'Causal Attributions During Therapy I: Responsibility and Blame', *Journal of Family Therapy* 25 (2), 136–60.

Summit, R. (1983) 'The Child Abuse Accommodation Syndrome', *Child Abuse and Neglect* 7, 177–93.

Swan, V. (1998) 'Narrative Therapy, Feminism and Race', in Seu, I. B. and Heenan, M. C. (eds) *Feminism and Psychotherapy: Reflections on Contemporary Theories and Practices*, 30–41. London: Sage.

Todorov, T. (1990) *Facing the Extreme*. New York: Metropolitan.

Tomm, K. (1987) 'Interventive Interviewing: Part II. Reflexive Questioning as a Means to Enable Self-healing', *Family Process* 26, 167–83.

Tomm, K. (2002) 'Enabling Forgiveness and Reconciliation in Family Therapy', *The International Journal of Narrative Therapy and Community Work* 1, 65–9.

Tomm, K. and Govier, T. (2007) 'Acknowledgement: Its Significance for Reconciliation and Wellbeing', in Flaskas, C., McCarthy, I. and Sheehan, J. (eds) *Hope and Despair in Narrative and Family Therapy*, 139–50. London: Routledge.

Traynor, C. (1998) 'Social Work in a Sectarian Society', in Anderson, M., Bogues, S. Campbell, J., Douglas, H. and McColgan, M. (eds) *Social Work and Social Change in Northern Ireland: Issues for Contemporary Practice*. Belfast: CCETSW.

Trickey, D. (2009) A Meta-Analysis of Risk Factors for PTSD in Faculty for Children and Young People Annual BPS Conference 2009, Royal Holloway University of London.

Trickey, D. and Black, D. (2000) 'Long Term Psychiatric Effects of Trauma on Children', *Trauma* 2, 261–68.

Turner, B. and Rennell, T. (1995) *When Daddy Came Home: How Family Life Changed for Ever in 1945*. London: Pimlico.

Van der Kolk, B. (1994) 'The Body Keeps The Score: Memory and the Evolving Psychobiology of Post Traumatic Stress', *Harvard Review of Psychiatry* 1(5), 253–65.

Van der Kolk, B., McFarlane, A. and Weisaeth, L. (1996) *Traumatic Stress: The Effects of Overwhelming Experience on Mind, Body, and Society*. London: Guilford.

Van der Kolk, B. (2009) 'Yoga and Post Traumatic Stress Disorder', *Integral Yoga Magazine*, Summer, 12–13.

Varela, F. (1979) *Principles of Biological Autonomy*. New York: North Holland.

Varela, F. (2001) 'Intimate Distances – Fragments for a Phenomenology of Organ Transplantation', *Journal of Consciousness Studies* 8, No. 5–7, 259–71.

Verhaeghe, P. (2004) *On Being Normal and Other Disorders: A Manual for Clinical Psychodiagnostics*. New York: Other Press.

Vickers, S. (2007) 'Once Upon a Life', *The Guardian*, 18 December 2007.

Von Bertalanfy, L. (1968) *General System Theory: Foundations, Development, Applications* (revised edition 1976). New York: George Braziller.

Vulliamy, E. (2010) Terezín: Music from a Nazi Ghetto, *The Observer*, 13 June 2010, 18

Wade, A. (2007) 'Despair, Resistance, Hope: Response-based Therapy with Victims of Violence', in Flaskas, C., McCarthy, I. and Sheehan, J. (eds) *Hope and Despair in Narrative and Family Therapy*, 63–75. London: Routledge.

Waldegrave, C. and Tamasese, K. (1993) 'Some Central Ideas in the "Just Therapy" Approach', *Australian and New Zealand Journal of Family Therapy* 14, 1–8

Walsh, F. (2002) 'A Family Resilience Framework: Innovative Practice Applications', *Family Relations*, Vol. 51 Issue 2, 130–8.

Walsh, F. (2008) *Spiritual Resource in Family Therapy* (2nd edition). London: Guilford.

Watzlawick, P., Weakland, J. H. and Fisch, R. (1974) *Change: The Principles of Problem Formation and Problem Resolution*. New York: W. W. Norton.

Weil, S. (1940) *The Iliad or the Poem of Force* (Critical Edition 2006). Translated by James P. Holoka. New York: Peter Lang.

White, M. (1995) *Re-Authoring Lives: Interviews and Essays*. Adelaide: Dulwich Centre.

White, M. B. and Russell, C. S. (1997) 'Examining the Multifaceted Notion of Isomorphism in Marriage and Family Therapy Supervision: A Quest for Conceptual Clarity', *Journal of Marital and Family Therapy* 23, 315–33.

White, M. (2005a) 'Children, Trauma and Subordinate Storyline Development', *The International Journal of Narrative Therapy and Community Work*, 3 and 4.

White, M. (2005b) *Narrative Practice and Exotic Lives: Resurrecting Diversity in Everyday Life*. Adelaide: Dulwich Centre.

Wilkomirski, B. (1995) *Fragments: Memories of a Wartime Childhood*. New York: Schocken.

Wilson, J. (2007) *The Performance of Practice: Enhancing the Repertoire of Therapy with Children and Families*. London: Karnac.

Yehuda, R. *et al.* (1998a) 'Vulnerability to Posttraumatic Stress Disorder in Adult Offspring of Holocaust Survivors', *American Journal of Psychiatry* 155, 1163–71.

Yehuda, R. *et al.* (1998b) 'Relationship Between Posttraumatic Stress Disorder Characteristics of Holocaust Survivors and Their Adult Offspring', *American Journal of Psychiatry* 155, 841–3.

Young, A. (2002) 'The Self Traumatised Perpetrator as a "Transient Mental Illness"', *L'Evolution Psychiatrique* 67, 630–50.

Young, A. (2007) 'Posttraumatic Stress Disorder of the Virtual Kind', in Sarat, A., Davidovitch, N. and Albertstein, M. (eds) *Trauma and Memory*, 21–48. Stanford CA: Stanford University Press.

INDEX

Page numbers in **bold type** refer to the glossary. *Italicised* page numbers refer to information that can be found in figures and tables. Abbreviation 'PTSD' is used for post traumatic stress disorder.